PRAISE FOR

Radical Friendship

"A skilled, natural storyteller and teacher, Kate generously shares her humanity and journey of fears, tears, and awakening as a mixed-race Dharma student, activist, and teacher. This is a rare opportunity to receive the gift of deeper understanding of a multilayered, heartbreaking, and heartwarming journey accompanied by integrated wisdom."

—GINA SHARPE

"*Radical Friendship* connects the Buddhist teachings to universal human experience by unraveling the narrow bandwidth of white supremacy within Western interpreted and colonized dharma. A radical teacher that lifts veils of privilege, oppression, and fragility (greed, hatred, delusion), this book invites and allows the dharma to permeate into all of our diverse lives that matter."

—LARRY YANG, author of *Awakening Together: The Spiritual Practice of Inclusivity and Community*

"*Radical Friendship* is a wise, ennobling, sanctuary of a book. It invites our heart to go deep into friendship, justice, love, and conscience. It reminds us of the beauty we can create with one another."

—JACK KORNFIELD, author of *A Path with Heart*

"With love and rigor, Kate Johnson offers a timely roadmap for healing and transformation. Through fierce honesty, compelling storytelling, and trauma-informed practices, she reminds us how to build relationship across difference and find freedom in every moment. I'm so glad she wrote this book."

—DAVID TRELEAVEN, PHD, author of *Trauma-Sensitive Mindfulness*

"This is a thoughtful and compassionate exploration of the meaning of friendship and its practice in today's confused and contentious world. Basing her exposition on an ancient Buddhist text, Kate Johnson offers us many precious nuggets of practical wisdom that can enrich our spiritual life, deepen personal relationships, and sustain us in ways that are both profoundly meaningful and fulfilling."

—VEN. BHIKKHU BODHI

"*Radical Friendship* has arrived on time! This book is relevant, on point, and apropos for the world we are living in today. Kate Johnson has provided a thought-provoking synthesis of Buddhist understanding and the politics of social justice, race, class, gender, ableism, and sexual orientation. She points to the many ways we might honor the spaces we occupy through identity without interpreting our differences as further proof that we are separate. She invites us to understand what freedom could be possible by applying this to relationship. Her perfectly chosen words and bigness of heart point us toward clear comprehension of what is possible if only we surrender and let go into the perfection of love—love for ourselves and love for others, buoyed by compassion, equanimity, and courage."

—DARA WILLIAMS

"In *Radical Friendship*, Kate Johnson examines the Buddha's teaching on the seven qualities a true spiritual friend should embody. The book describes her journey as she sets out to become a true friend to herself and others. Johnson offers a fresh and timely interpretation of spiritual friendship informed by her study, her practice, and life experiences."

—SHARON SALZBERG, author of *Real Happiness*

RADICAL FRIENDSHIP

7 Ways to Love Yourself
and Find Your People
in an Unjust World

KATE JOHNSON

SHAMBHALA

Shambhala Publications, Inc.
2129 13th Street
Boulder, Colorado 80302
www.shambhala.com

Cover art: Signet/Shutterstock and LivDeco/Shutterstock
Cover design: Daniel Urban-Brown
Interior design: Kate Huber-Parker

9 8 7 6 5 4 3 2

Printed in the United States of America

♾ This edition is printed on acid-free paper that meets the
American National Standards Institute Z39.48 Standard.
♻ Shambhala Publications makes every effort to print on recycled
paper. For more information please visit www.shambhala.com.

Shambhala Publications is distributed worldwide by
Penguin Random House, Inc., and its subsidiaries.

Library of Congress Cataloging-in-Publication Data
Names: Johnson, Kate, 1981–
Title: Radical friendship: seven ways to love yourself and
find your people in an unjust world / Kate Johnson.
Description: Boulder, Colorado: Shambhala Publications, Inc., 2021.
Identifiers: LCCN 2020001496 | ISBN 9781611808117 (trade paperback)
Subjects: LCSH: Interpersonal relations. |
Self-acceptance. | Relationship quality.
Classification: LCC HM1106 .J648 2021 | DDC 302—dc23
LC record available at https://lccn.loc.gov/2020001496

To my mother, Ann

&

my daughter Maple

CONTENTS

PRACTICES

Introduction

This is a book about finding your freedom, finding your people, and the possibility that these are actually two parts of one and the same spiritual path.

It's a book about friendship as both a fundamental human relationship and a fundamental attitude of heart and mind with which we can navigate the world around us. Friendship as an inner fulcrum upon which all our actions can reliably hinge, a compass to offer us direction when we're lost, and a shield to protect us.

This is also a guide to reopening spaces for collective friendship, even friendship at the societal level. Of course, whenever we are relating to another human being or community, we are bridging a difference of some kind. Our survival in an unjust world will depend on our capacity to be, feel, and move in right relationship with all various backgrounds, identities, and lived experiences that exist within us and between us.

The idea for writing this book began, as all growing things do, with a seed—in this case, a talk at a Buddhist conference in spring 2013. The event had come under fire in the previous year for promising audiences "the emerging face of Buddhism in the West," and delivering a roster of speakers that was almost entirely white and male. In the following year, the organizers were doing their best to make things right by increasing the number of presenters who were women and people of color. I was one of them.

Just a few months earlier, while I was on a two-month silent Buddhist meditation retreat, a Black teenager named Michael Brown was shot and killed in Ferguson, Missouri, by a white police officer, Darren Wilson. Because I'd given up reading, writing, and talking while away on retreat in deep solitary practice, I'd had no conscious knowledge of what had happened. But in my meditations over those two months, I experienced terror like I had never known before. I was so fearful, I could hardly put one foot in front of the other to leave my room. I figured it was some sort of purification, a release of all the unmetabolized fear I've felt in my life, and the fears of all the generations before me that feed into this one. It wasn't a bad way to make sense of things, and maybe not even a wrong way, but I know now that it wasn't the whole story. I believe I was sensing in to something much bigger than myself.

On the ride to the bus station on my way home from the retreat, my taxi driver informed me. I heard Michael Brown's name for the first time, and learned that he had been unarmed, murdered, his body left bleeding in the street for hours. For the people of Ferguson, Missouri, who had been terrorized by white supremacist police officers for decades, who had seen countless family members, friends, and loved ones beaten or killed by those officers,

Brown's death was a breaking point. When the Black residents of Ferguson went out into the streets to express their grief, they were assaulted with tear gas and rubber bullets by police officers in riot gear. Activists, artists, healers, and others from around the country had gathered to support the mourning community in Ferguson and to defend Black lives. The events that unfolded after that murder exposed to the world what some Americans had already known or suspected: the illusion of a post-racial society was exactly that.

As all this was unfolding, I had been sitting in silence for months somewhere in Massachusetts, trying to gather my mind. On that taxi ride to the bus station, the irony hit me. I had originally started meditating to deal with multiple sources of stress, not the least of which was the pervasive stress of being a mixed-race Black person in a violently racist society. I *kept* meditating because the practice had begun to heal the suffering of separation I felt inside—the separation from myself, from the people I had loved, and from the world around me.

And yet, there was something fundamentally isolating about the approach to practice that I had been taught at the meditation centers where I'd trained. Centers that were all predominantly white. Even in meditation spaces full of people in the heart of New York City, we rarely talked to each other either before or after class. At the rural center where I'd practiced for weeks and months at time on several occasions, we were instructed not even to look at each other during our retreat. Teachers sometimes spoke about our personal practices of peacefulness contributing to the liberation of all beings everywhere. I loved this language and found it inspiring, but at the time, I didn't see meditation communities doing a whole lot to put this language into practice. The rhetoric was expansive, but cultures of those meditation retreat spaces were far more narrow: in the Western-convert Buddhism that I had been practicing, spiritual liberation was an individual affair.

I was deeply grateful for the transformative meditation practices I had learned at those centers, and I also knew that what they offered was not everything I needed to get to the deep freedom I dreamed of. As the uprising that affirmed Black Lives Matter swelled and blossomed, it became so very clear to me that if our meditation practices weren't actively liberating us from white dominance and other forms of oppression, they would very soon cease to be relevant. Collective liberation wasn't going to happen in silos where solitude and silence are the norms. To achieve freedom from structural violence in society, we would need to begin using our personal practices as the foundation for wise relationships within our communities. And frankly, the Buddhist communities I was a part of were failing at that. I had been harmed, had witnessed harm, and had probably harmed others countless times in these well-meaning spaces. For all our talk of mindfulness, compassion, and liberation for all beings, the supremacy that pervaded these communities remained somewhat unspeakable and largely unaddressed.

I knew I wanted to deliver this message at the Buddhist Geeks Conference, but I was terrified to say these things to the still mostly white, mostly male audience there. I knew the mere mention of racism made some white folks uncomfortable, and that discomfort could lead to unsavory reactions. My credentials could be called into question. My statistics could be challenged and torn apart. I could be dismissed—not because I was wrong, but because they didn't like what I had to say. I spent most of my preparatory hours trying to find the right words, the right voice, the right stance, so that my listeners would actually hear me. It was a tremendous labor to try to put myself into their perspective, to try to see myself through their eyes, to anticipate how my message would land.

I opened by saying this:

I'm thinking about [this talk] as one statement in a conversation that for some of us is ongoing. For some of us, we're just kind of jumping into the conversation right now. *I'm talking to you not as an expert, but as a friend,* as a community member, as someone who cares . . .[1]

As a friend, I spoke about mindfulness practice as a tool for waking up to implicit bias—the kind of snap judgment that could lead a police officer to murder an unarmed child. I quoted studies, I offered up my own experiences, and I made the case that waking up to the dynamics of power and oppression, in ourselves and in our communities, is a profound spiritual practice in its own right. I shared my conviction that, as practitioners of Buddhist meditation, our training could uniquely position us to uproot racial bias and other forms of delusion—if we were willing to apply our practice to those particular forms of suffering. I expressed my disappointment that together, we had unintentionally created spiritual gated communities that were more about staying comfortable than becoming free.

To my amazement, the conference-goers were totally into it. As that morning's session concluded, dozens of people formed a spontaneous breakout group to continue the conversation about undoing racism and other forms of oppression, both in our spiritual communities and in ourselves. I joined the circle in the hopes of listening in. Eventually, the group turned back to me, looking for answers.

"What do we *do*?" they wanted to know.

"Let your hearts break," I told them. I wanted them to stop and feel—not to rush into action before truly absorbing the scope of the current reality of which many of them had just scratched the surface.

Their questions, though, remained alive in my mind. What *is* the practice that can wake us up to the dynamics of privilege and oppression that exist within us and between us? How *do* we ever connect authentically across the differences that our society has so painfully divided us by?

WHY FRIENDSHIP?

When I was approached by an editor to write a book based on the talk I gave at the conference, I knew the appropriate response was yes. First of all, that's just what you're supposed to say when someone asks you to write a book. But I also saw it as an opportunity to continue the conversation that had been unfinished at that Buddhist conference some years before. The short talk I gave had been mostly a call to action, a request for that particular (mostly white, mostly male) audience to apply their mindfulness practices to dismantling racism and other forms of oppression at the level of thought and perception. But, I knew there was so much more to explore in terms of the actual practice of liberating relationships—in our words, behavior, and community culture. In my teaching life, I had been exploring the possibilities of the Buddha's teachings on spiritual friendship as a framework to support this activity of showing up for each other's freedom—spiritually, yes, but also socially and politically. Even in an unjust world. Even across difference. Even after generations and generations of harm.

What I didn't know was how much the writing of this text would put me through the wringer of deeply examining my own friendships with individuals and relationships with communities over the years. In the writing, I began to recognize what a profound impact living in societal structures marked by violence and domination had on my capacity to connect with other people, and also with myself. I also began to recognize just how personal my obsession with friendship is, and why those questions from the white conference attendees would not leave me alone.

The first time I learned that my race could be the site of separation between me and the people I loved, I was four years old, surrounded by plastic toys floating in warm suds. My mother was rinsing my hair by submerging a bowl under the water to fill it, lifting it up, and supporting my neck while she poured it over my tipped-back head.

"Mom, am I Black or white?"

No response. I wiped my eyes to clear away any shampoo bubbles before I opened them. In my memory, my mother was still, her neck held long and stiff, and the rinsing bowl was hovering midair.

"Who asked you that question?"

"A girl at school," I replied. We had been playing side by side on the swings. She had leaped off at the top of one particularly big swing, flying briefly through the air before landing on all fours, wood chips flying everywhere. A highly respected playground move. She turned, made a funny face, and we laughed and laughed.

When we stopped giggling, she asked if I was Black or white. I didn't know. She told me she needed to know whether or not she could be friends with me, so I should go home and find out and let her know tomorrow.

My mother laid her forearm over the rim of the tub as she listened and rested her head on it. I twirled her silky hair in my small hand.

"You're not Black *or* white," she murmured. "You're tan. You're beautiful. And you can play with whomever you want."

Now, I might have been only four, but I knew that "tan" wasn't a thing. It *definitely* wasn't a thing I could take back to that Chicago playground in the early 1980s. Not a thing that would give me or anyone else a sense of who I was and where I belonged. I could see that this question of Black or white was one that stressed my mother out, one that she didn't have answers for, so I didn't ask any more questions. I was a Black biracial child growing up in a violently segregated city. I had a Black Honduran father and a white American mother who were desperately trying to shield me from the fiction of race and the fact of racism that was all around us. Even on the swing set. I did my best to let them.

In the end, I don't remember what I told the little girl back at school or whether we ended up playing together. I do remember what I learned from her, though: Some of my lighter-skinned classmates were being told by their families, even at that early age, not to hang out with Black girls. I learned that we live in a world where skin color matters and where our friendships might depend on it. And, I learned that being honest about my experiences navigating a racist world would only upset some people— though I didn't yet know why.

In time, I discovered that for some people, my light-brown skin was actually *the* standard of beauty. They assumed I was smarter and more trustworthy than darker-skinned people, and I was given attention and opportunities because of it. For others, my skin was a threat. Being neither white nor Black enough was reason enough to be bullied and left out. Through my later childhood years and into my early teens, my confusion about who I was and where I belonged made it difficult for me to make real, deep friendships. When you're constantly pondering the neither/nor, betwixt-and-betweenness of your racial heritage, it's pretty hard to be present with other people. My default settings were (1) guarding against rejection and (2) feeling I had something to prove. Around the same time, my parents' interracial, cross-cultural, cross-class relationship sputtered and failed. I wondered what that meant about me.

This book ended up with much more of me in it than I originally intended. While the stories are personal, I know that they are far from unique. My intention in including them is twofold. First, I want you to know me. I want you to know where I'm coming from and to be honest about having a point of view and sharing from it. Second, I hope even if you don't relate to the details of my experiences, they might inspire you to reflect on your own life and stories in a way that moves you closer to being free. The more closely I look, the more I recognize just how mixed many of us are—and I'm not just talking about race. When it comes to gender, sexuality, class, abilities and disabilities, likes and dislikes, and personalities, we are hardly ever just one thing. True friendship can be a space of rediscovering the idiosyncrasies and complexities within ourselves and in loving relationship with one another. What can be known from that place of celebrating inner multiplicity? And, how can that practice lead us into even better, more liberated friendships?

LINEAGE

My own first liberation teachings came not from the Buddha but from feminist writers of color. In my late teens, I spent hours wandering bookstores and libraries looking for a reflection of myself that I recognized, that I felt I could claim. I found it in the writings of bell hooks, Audre Lorde, Gloria Anzaldúa, Sandra Cisneros, and Patricia Hill Collins, among many others. I'd always thought of oppression as something that my ancestors had experienced and participated in (both sides, different ways), but not as a term that could be used to describe my own present-day lived experience. Through the windows of their words, I finally saw a language for describing the systems of supremacy that I had experienced all my life, a language that could help me understand how these systems moved within and shaped me. In most of my social interactions, I'd gotten into the habit of holding myself tightly, narrowly. I was bracing against a constant pressure, bracing against the inevitable look of confusion or disdain, careful not to take up too much space. As I developed a structural analysis of my lived experiences, I gradually began to slow down, spread out, and connect with more confidence with the world around me.

Moreover, these texts by feminists of color articulated ways of being that I hadn't quite known were possible before I read them, but that I immediately recognized as *liberated*. I'll never forget cracking open *In Search of Our Mothers' Gardens*, Alice Walker's book of essays, and reading this definition:

WOMANIST

1. From womanish. (Opp. of "girlish," i.e., frivolous, irresponsible, not serious.) A black feminist or feminist of color. From the black folk expression of mothers to female children, "you acting womanish," i.e., like a woman. Usually referring to outrageous, audacious, courageous, or willful behavior. Wanting to know more and in greater depth than is considered "good" for one. Interested in grown up doings. Acting grown up. Being grown up. Interchangeable with another black folk expression: "You trying to be grown." Responsible. In charge. Serious.

2. Also: A woman who loves other women, sexually and/or nonsexually. Appreciates and prefers women's culture, women's emotional flexibility (values tears as natural counterbalance of laughter), and women's strength. Sometimes loves individual men, sexually and/or nonsexually. Committed to survival and wholeness of entire people, male and female. Not a separatist, except periodically, for health. Traditionally a universalist, as in: "Mama, why are we brown, pink, and yellow, and our cousins are white, beige, and black?" Ans. "Well, you know the colored race is just like a flower garden, with every color flower represented." Traditionally capable, as in: "Mama, I'm walking to Canada and I'm taking you and a bunch of other slaves with me." Reply: "It wouldn't be the first time."

3. Loves music. Loves dance. Loves the moon. Loves the Spirit. Loves love and food and roundness. Loves struggle. Loves the Folk. Loves herself. Regardless.

4. Womanist is to feminist as purple is to lavender.[2]

It was 1983 when Walker wrote this, and some of the language is a little binary, but I hope you can feel what I felt in her intent. In her definition, I saw a vision of my future self: rich and vivid and bold and whole. I knew I needed to go in the direction of embodying my own maturity; embracing my seriousness; loving my race, gender, and sexuality; loving the world; and enjoying all the good things in it. I just didn't know exactly how to get there.

It was then that I caught my second wave of liberation lessons, in the form of the Buddha's teachings, which provided a series of road maps to the kind of self-love and love for the world and its people that I wanted to embody completely. I'd always been contemplative and spiritually precocious. At four, I loved to sit in windowsills and watch dust particles gleam and dance in the sunlight. At ten years old I was a witchy, dreamy kid who could often be found making potions out of leaves and stones from the backyard. I used to go down to our basement and hole up with a dusty copy of the *Encyclopedia of World Religions*, studying the pictures before I could really understand the text.

After surveying the various options for many years, at the age of eleven, I decided I was probably a Buddhist. I shoplifted *The Tibetan Book of The Dead* from my local

Barnes &Noble and continued to study various texts on my own. But it wasn't until my early twenties that I sought out formal instructions and teachers who could guide me on the path. I feel especially grateful for my teachers, some of whom have become my friends: especially Gina Sharpe, Larry Yang, Lila Kate Wheeler, Arawana Hayashi, Thanissara, Kittisaro, Lama Rod Owens, and Ethan Nichtern. I offer a deep bow to the Asian ancestors of these traditions, who are not my own ancestors, but whom I honor as if they were, as best I can.

The Buddhist teachings were very powerful for me because they offered concrete ways to develop the fullness and luminosity of heart and mind I aspire to express in this life. The teachings are practical—they suggest not only what to do but also *how* to do it, offering actionable tools I could apply while walking, talking, cooking, working, and resting, in addition to formal meditation practice. In the wake of the Ferguson uprisings, when I was desperate to find resources for a more relational practice of liberation within this body of teachings I was so devoted to. While most of the mindfulness courses popular today emphasize silent sitting meditation practices, meditation instructions actually make up a very small percentage of the Buddha's teachings. One monk I spoke with estimated that at least 90 percent of the texts in the Pali Canon, where the early teachings are found, are stories about being in relationship, stories that teach us how to be with each other in the most enlightened way possible.

One of my favorite stories illustrating the importance of friendship, and the possibilities for freedom within it, appears in the *Upaddha Sutta*, a record of a conversation between the Buddha and his cousin and fellow monk, the venerable Ananda. It begins with Ananda making this declaration:

> This is fully *half* of the holy life, lord: admirable friendship, admirable companionship, admirable camaraderie.

Ananda probably thought this was a bold statement to make. Provocative, even. But in this story, the Buddha raises him one.

> Don't say that, Ananda. Don't say that. Admirable friendship, admirable companionship, admirable camaraderie is actually the *whole* of the holy life.[3]

Oppression is fundamentally fragmenting. It stresses our capacity to connect with one another. And it keeps us so busy fighting to survive that we lack the time and the emotional bandwidth to sustain the friendships we already have or to reach out and form new ones. So, when I read the Buddha's assertion that admirable friendship is the *whole* of the holy life, I hear him saying that friendship is the medicine for the isolation we often feel within supremacist societies. In a climate like this, friendship is not a detour or roadside decoration on our journey to liberation. It is a direct pathway to embodying freedom, collectively, in this very moment.

For me, radical friendship is the practice of developing the inner spiritual capacities that allow us to show up for our own liberation and the expression of these capacities in all of our relationships as we show up for each other. I see friendship as the base unit of relationship within families, communities, and larger societal structures. I believe the skills that we build in showing up for each other in radical friendship will also help us build social movements, transform political power, bridge splits, recover losses, repair wounds, and share joy.

At that conference way back when, in the talk that sparked the writing of this book, I spoke about how white people could apply Buddhist practices to liberating their minds and hearts from white supremacy. I used myself as an example, as if to say: "Look, white people. Even *I* have internalized white supremacy, and if I have to deal with it, then so do you." I did it in the name of friendship, and a lot of people said it helped them. But, the energetic cost of talking to white people about race, of forcing myself into a shape that I hoped would be palatable for them—all of this work didn't register at the time. It was a labor I had gotten used to.

Whenever we make something big and visible—an artwork, a project, a book—it always ends up containing both the things we intended to build into it—and the things that we didn't. The first few drafts of *Radical Friendship* had a nagging tendency to center whiteness, a hangover from my many years of schooling and working in predominantly white institutions. A friend who read an earlier version asked me point-blank: "Is this really the book you want to write?" Thank God for good friends. I do want this book to be about more than surviving white supremacy (though I do, of course, intend for all of us survive it). And, I definitely want it to be about more than teaching white people how to be better friends. Writing from that place feels like speaking out of an old story.

So I began again, with the intention to center the experience that I know best, because I live it: the experience of carrying both privileged and oppressed identities, of navigating friendships across a variety of ever-changing terrains in an unjust world, and of somehow managing to forge relationships rooted in love and trust in spite of these conditions. Or maybe even because of them.

The practice of radical friendship requires that we tell ourselves a new story: we don't have to choose between being loved and being true to ourselves. Whatever our past experiences with friendship have been, and however we have participated in them, we can mine those experiences for wisdom and growth with awareness and love. Every single one of us has made mistakes in our friendships, or harmed ourselves or others out of ignorance or fear. We've all been burned in friendship too—disrespected, underappreciated, or left out. A radical friendship reminds us that we are always worthy of love, we can always heal, and we can always change. It's a story I know well, but my voice sometimes cracks when I tell it.

Here's to you and me telling it anyway.

(1)

Friendship as Freedom

Monks, a friend endowed with seven
   qualities is worth associating with.

Which seven?

They give what is hard to give.
They do what is hard to do.
They endure what is hard to endure.
They reveal their secrets to you.
They keep your secrets.
When misfortunes strike, they don't
   abandon you.
When you're down and out, they don't
   look down on you.

A friend endowed with these seven
   qualities is worth associating with.
                 —*Mitta Sutta*

THIS PASSAGE COMES from a longer body of the Buddha's teachings called the *Anguttara Nikaya.*[4] Sutta means
"thread" in the ancient Indian language of Pali. I don't remember where I first heard the thread of wisdom that is

the *Mitta Sutta*, but I remember that when I did, I instantly knew three things.

1. I wanted to be that kind of friend.
2. I wanted to *have* that kind of friend.
3. Nothing in my experience or education had adequately prepared me for either of these things.

The relationship described in the text is referred to as *kalyana mitta*—spiritual friendship. In some Buddhist traditions, this phrase refers to the committed relationship between a teacher and student. The Buddha actually referred to himself as a spiritual friend on several occasions. But kalyana mitta is also the name for the quality of relationships between members of a community who are collectively committed to liberation. It's a beautiful invitation to regard our friends, and our friendships, as our teachers. In this book, I'm exploring spiritual friendship mostly in this second sense—the relationships between equals that lead to freedom, and accompany us along the way.

I use the term *radical*, rather than *spiritual*, to describe the friendship in the *Mitta Sutta* because the word spiritual often conveys a sense of transcendent otherworldliness. *Radical*, by contrast, means "of or relating to the roots." By radical friendship, I mean the kind of friendship that has the potential to heal us at the very ground of our being. Wounds from when we were young; maybe even wounds from before we were born. The kind of friendship that forges bonds so strong that systems of oppression can't break them. The kind of friendship that helps us gather enough power and love that we can profoundly transform ourselves and the world.

In my mind, radical friendship need not even be limited to the people we currently think of as friends. We can practice these principles with our neighbors and colleagues, our children and elders, the people we serve and the people who serve us. Our people, as it turns out, are all around us. We find them by becoming the kind of friends that we ourselves would like to have.

This book borrows its structure from the Buddha's instructions on friendship in the *Mitta Sutta*, which can be found at the beginning of this chapter. Each of the following chapters explores one line of that text and the core contemplation it calls us into, with practices for action and reflection in our modern, everyday lives. But first, some notes on the practice of radical friendship in the closest relationship we will ever have.

MAKING FRIENDS WITH OURSELVES

Meditation is making friends with yourself. It's a statement that struck me as hokey when I first heard it, but the more I practice, the more profound it seems. Truth be told, there are things I've said to myself that I would never, ever say to a friend. I've flaked on my own self-care dates, broken promises of rest and quality time, and pushed myself too hard by telling myself that my best wasn't good enough.

I've forced myself to be silent when I wanted to speak. I've scolded myself for being sick or tired, and refused myself the opportunity to ask for help. Basically, I've had moments of treating myself like someone I didn't even like, let alone love.

What makes friendship with ourselves so radical is that we dare to do it in a world where the dominant culture would rather we be at war with ourselves. In *The Body Is Not an Apology*, author and activist Sonya Renee Taylor names this pervasive force of cruelty toward ourselves as a paradigm of "body terrorism" in the Western world. "Our economic systems," she writes, "shape how we see our bodies and the bodies of others, and they ultimately inform what we are compelled to do or buy based on that reflection."[5] In other words, self-hatred is a big business. Radical self-love, Taylor proposes, can heal the harms caused by misogyny, ageism, fatphobia, and ableism, among other oppressive ideologies. If we think our bodies are actually OK, if we're kind to them—feeding them when they're hungry, accepting them even when they can't do something they used to do, understanding that they sometimes get sick and eventually get old, dressing them in a way that makes *us* feel fabulous and happy anyway—then we don't need to build our worth through products and services. So often, the things we buy don't fill the void anyway.

Meditation is making friends with yourself. How many of us can truly say we are our own best friend? I know I mentioned in the introduction that meditation alone is not enough to undo the conditioning that has been perpetuated by systems of injustice. It's also true that meditation can *be a part of* the healing process for those of us who have been deeply harmed by these systems. The key is not making meditation yet another way to beat up on ourselves for not being good enough. Meditating from the belief that we are broken and need to be fixed will only undermine our efforts to develop calm and ease. Self-aggression squeezes the mind, and discursive, aggressive thoughts spill out everywhere. Meditation, at its best, is an offering of love to ourselves. It gets even better with practice.

I learned this lesson in a big way once, while practicing on yet another three-month silent meditation retreat. I'd quietly decided before I arrived that I would do it "the hard way." Which meant acting on a subtle belief that being mentally brutal with myself was the best way to swiftly spur myself toward enlightenment. At the end of each day, I felt mentally fatigued and physically sore. Still, I soldiered on, paying attention to mind moment after mind moment with obsessive dedication. After one particularly long and uncompromising day of following the retreat schedule to the minute and cramming in extra meditation sessions during mealtimes, I was crossing the threshold from the meditation room to the hallway when I heard an inner voice comment: *Not good enough.* It felt like a tiny jab.

In the short walk from the meditation hall back to the dormitory, I noticed that voice chiming in at least a half dozen times. Walking: *not slow enough.* Stopping on the way to my room to get some tea: *not focused enough.* Putting honey into said tea: *not hardcore enough.* Every action I took seemed to provoke this harsh inner commentary. I realized that the internal criticisms had been coming for quite some time, only they were so subtle and familiar I hadn't noticed them. I heard them, but they appeared in my mind as if they were simply the truth. Each comment only hurt a bit, like a pinprick. But, at the end of a day of being pricked every few moments, I was aching and full of holes.

When I shared this experience in a meeting with the guiding teacher on that retreat, he suggested that I relate to this inner voice as if it were coming from a cartoon character. Externalizing it, picturing the voice coming from something I could have a sense of humor about, might help me at least tolerate the experience, since I couldn't control it. Because each criticism felt like a sharp jab, I nicknamed this inner critic "Jabba the Hutt." I'd never actually seen *Star Wars* at the time (I know, I know), so I imagined Jabba looking something like Marvin the Martian—a tiny knight perched on my shoulder who jabbed me with a sharp staff from time to time.

My teacher advised me to be really aware of when the mind state I now called Jabba was present and to reflect on whether it had some purpose it was trying to serve. When I dropped that question into my mind—*Is Jabba trying to help me?*—the answer felt clear as a bell. Being hard on myself had worked so beautifully in so many other areas of my life; I'd managed to exceed society's expectations, to be regarded in schools and workplaces as impressive, exceptional. Mastering Buddhist meditation, I thought, should be just like conquering any other obstacle that I'd blasted through up until this point.

Turns out, I couldn't just put my head down and bulldoze my way to nirvana. When I tried to flick Jabba off my shoulder and go back to my breath, or when I spent an entire practice period inwardly yelling at him to push off, he just came back. Jabbing with a flourish, he whisper-screamed a defiant *Not good enough!* inside my mind.

At some point, I said to this inner voice, *Listen. I understand that you're trying to help me. But what you're doing—it's not helping right now. I'm already doing the best I can. So, why don't you just come sit with me while I watch my breath?* I imagined pulling the angry little guy into my lap, tucking him under my arm, and putting a blanket over him. From time to time, Jabba would stir and get rowdy, and I would soothe him again: *It's OK. We're doing fine. Just a few more minutes, just like this. One breath at a time.*

Sitting with Jabba seemed like such a humble use of this meditation retreat. I wasn't busting through any new dimensions of consciousness, I thought, or dissolving my ego into pure bliss. I was just sitting there, calming an imaginary enemy that wouldn't let me get into the real meditation. Oddly enough, when I gave in and treated myself and Jabba (who was, of course, also me) with kindness, I found that I did not end up plagued by a dumb cartoon character for the remainder of the retreat. I spent a good few days offering friendship and understanding to the voice inside me that told me I wasn't good enough, and after turning to face it with love in my heart, it started to soften and subside all on its own. It was as if, by committing to making friends with that cranky, critical part of my own mind, it no longer had anything to poke at or stick to. The experience also yielded great insights into the nature of self and consciousness, by the way. Insights I don't believe I ever could have found if I hadn't given up fighting my experience and started allowing it to be, dropping the struggle and trying my best to love it even when I didn't like it.

The reason why making friends with ourselves is so essential on the path to liberation is that the forces of privilege and oppression are not just out there in the world somewhere. We've all inhaled harmful societal messages and unknowingly integrated them into the most intimate structures of our bodies and minds, where they manifest in a seemingly personal way. Perfectionism is just one example. In their classic manual *Dismantling Racism: A Workbook for Social Change Groups*, anti-oppression trainers Tema Okun and Kenneth Jones wrote about the perfectionism that manifests in unjust systems as "the failure to appreciate our own and others' good work." We can recognize it, they suggest, through the presence of a "harsh and constant inner critic" that points out our faults, failures, inadequacies, and mistakes in a way that makes it nearly impossible to actually learn from them.[6]

Okun and Jones identified chronic perfectionism as just one of the characteristics of "white supremacy culture"—the expression of which isn't limited to skinheads and the Ku Klux Klan. It's a set of ideologies that can be perpetuated by *anyone* acculturated within societies that systematically advantage white people to the disadvantage of Black, Indigenous, and other people of color. Their complete list of characteristics of white supremacy culture also includes:

- **Perfectionism:** identifying self and other with mistakes, little appreciation for assets
- **Sense of urgency:** the drive for quick and visible results
- **Defensiveness:** an inability to tolerate feedback or criticism
- **Valuing quantity over quality:** if results can't be measured, they have no value
- **Worship of the written word:** little respect for other ways information is shared
- **Paternalism:** lack of clarity around how power is held and decisions are made
- **Either/or thinking:** oversimplifying complexity and creating false binaries
- **Power hoarding:** little value around sharing power at the level of leadership
- **Fear of open conflict:** those who raise issues are seen as problematic or innappropriate
- **Individualism:** a culture of competition instead of collaboration, leads to isolation
- **Progress = bigger and more:** an appetite for growth without considering impacts of continuous expansion
- **Belief in objectivity:** a premium on logic and reason, privileging what can be known through the mind, invalidating expressions of emotion[7]

You probably see where I'm going with this. So many of the norms of white supremacy that are observable in our organizational and community cultures can *also* be seen at the microlevel in our meditation practices—because, if you're like me, you probably learned to meditate within the dominant cultural paradigm. This culture reinforces a sense of urgency to get somewhere in our meditation practice. Valuing quantity over quality by competing or comparing with others about how many minutes we meditate for. Engaging in either/or thinking by approaching the practice as if there is only one right way or obsessing about which lineage is the best. Reinforcing individualism by approaching spiritual practice primarily as a solitary pursuit, preferring an app over a relationship with a teacher and a community. The sad fact is that these values, so normalized and even prized within white supremacy culture, actually *undermine* our spiritual progress, and they usually make us miserable in the process.

Here's the good news though: in our meditation practice, we can hardly help but see these characteristics arise in us if we're willing to honestly look. Recognizing them for what they are (forms of suffering) and establishing a new relationship with them (the wish to let go) sets us firmly on the path to dismantling them for good. Meditation itself is a practice that can help us to heal these tendencies and develop new ones that don't rely on violence and domination to help us grow.

Liberating our bodies, hearts, and minds from internalized oppression takes time, energy, and lots and lots of love.

We need to believe we are worth the effort. And, we need to find others who are in it for the journey too. Liberation is not, and was never meant to be, a solitary path. So, let's talk a little about what it takes to accompany each other on the journey.

BEYOND ALLY

I found myself in need of good company in spring 2015, when I was serving as the transformational activism coordinator for a small multilineage meditation center in New York City. I had become a dedicated community member and was quickly promoted to leadership in the organization, just as racial injustice and police brutality were rising into mainstream consciousness. The Movement for Black Lives was in full swing, and I found that the predominantly white community of students and teachers were looking to me—one of the few Black people in the community and the *only* one in leadership—for clues about how to respond to the political moment.

It's a lot of pressure, being the only one. My picture appeared all over the organization's website and newsletters, advertising a racial diversity that didn't yet exist in most of our classes. I worried constantly that my image would attract people of color to the space when I wasn't there, that they would have a bad experience, and they would be turned off from meditation for good. I felt responsible for making sure all the white teachers and leaders were educated in how to hold space for people who were different from them. These were impossible tasks, and I did a lot of unpaid (and sometimes unwelcome) "diversity consulting" as a result.

I had an unwavering trust in the power of mindfulness to help us awaken, and I was excited about the possibilities of what mindfulness could do when applied to our relationships, organizations, and institutions. I also knew that if mindfulness was our *only* tool for healing racism and other forms of institutional oppression, that healing would take a very, very long time. A lot of lifelong meditators and even teachers were profoundly awake in some ways, yet still very much asleep in this particular one. There was a social movement blooming all around us, and as a community, I felt that we were not well-equipped to join or even respond to it.

I joined forces with a few other freedom-minded students and together we developed programs that we hoped would help build the skills we needed, events that combined awareness, and compassion practices with political education about anti-oppression and social justice work. One of the events was a panel discussion called "What Is an Ally? Solidarity in the Sangha." "Ally" is the position we claim when we express our feelings of support for someone across a difference in lived experience, usually someone with less institutional power than we have. "*Sangha*" is a Pali word that's often translated as "the community of spiritual seekers."

Sangha is the third of a series of gifts that we gain access to on the dharma path, which are called the three jewels, the three gems, or the three refuges. Of the three, sangha often proves to be the most difficult to practice. The first gem or refuge is the Buddha: we are invited to hold as precious and take refuge in the example of the historical Buddha and all the enlightened beings, and also in our own innate capacity for liberation. The dharma, the second gem, is the body of teachings from the wisdom texts, as well as our direct observations of our lives and our world, that we can rely on for support and guidance. The sangha, however, is the one gem that requires us to be in relationship with other people, not just books or our own minds. And *people* are unpredictable. It can feel so risky to take refuge in community. Are these really *our* people? How do we know? How do we get and stay in right relationship with them? What will we do when one of us messes up? And of course, our core question for the "What is an Ally?" event: how do we find real solidarity with one another?

Four panelists appeared that night: Derek Cobb, a peer meditation guide at The Reciprocity Foundation for homeless youth; Dr. Crystal Fleming, an author, cultural critic, and professor of Africana Studies; Meredith Gray, an anti-racist educator and professional mediator; and Natalia Salgado, who was at the time the deputy director of 32BJ, the service workers' union that was powerfully supporting the "Fight for $15" fair wages campaign. Some of the people who showed up to hear them that night were existing community members, but many were new to the space, people who were looking for a spiritual home that didn't require they check their politics at the door.

Everyone in the room seemed interested in stretching the bounds of so-called "allyship" and transforming it into something even more authentic, relational, and real. We spoke about the elevation of allyship from a transactional relationship to a reciprocal one, in which everyone involved recognizes and enjoys the mutual benefit of being committed to one another. We discussed the role that mindfulness meditation can play in helping us recognize what we need from the people we are practicing (or organizing) with, and to develop the courage to articulate those needs. We reckoned with the truth that when there's a power differential in a relationship, one person has the authority to make the other comply with their wishes, and the other one does not. We spoke of our allyship fails and what we'd learned from them. About genuine relationships as a way to build power for societal transformation. About who we wanted to be, what we wanted to be a part of, and who we wanted to be *with* during the great political turning that seemed to be unfolding all around us.

Most Buddhist spaces (including the ones I belonged to) were profoundly conflict-avoidant. Sure, intellectual debate was encouraged. But, those who dared to point out a problem with the leadership or organizational culture were dismissed as if they were the ones who created the problem. That combination of fragility and scapegoating made it very hard to get to the actual problems, let alone to approach real solutions.

As I hosted the discussion that evening, it became clear to me just how many characteristics of white supremacy were deeply embedded within the culture of our particular organization, and within almost every institution of mindfulness, wellness, yoga, and Western Buddhism I had experienced. Looking back at Jones and Okun's list from *Dismantling Racism* after listening to the panel, I could really see how, despite our best intentions, there was both power hoarding and lack of clarity about who actually held power and how decisions were made. The characteristic of "worship of the written word" is particularly toxic within American Buddhism. In her essay "We've Been Here All Along," Dr. Funie Hsu outlines how Asian and Asian American Buddhist practitioners and teachers have been systematically excluded from publication by Western Buddhist publishing houses, while their white students have built careers as Buddhist leaders. She writes:

In mainstream white American Buddhist conversations, white Buddhists are often heralded as the erudite saviors and purifiers of Buddhism. This perspective exemplifies the subtle enactments and overwhelming hubris of white supremacy. In positioning a certain type of Buddhism (white) as better than other kinds of Buddhism (Asian, "folk," "baggage Buddhism"), the white ownership of Buddhism is claimed through delegitimizing the validity and long history of our traditions, then appropriating the practices on the pretext of performing them more correctly.[8]

In the voices of the attendees, and in my own heart, I heard the declaration that dismantling this culture was going to take more than what we understood as allyship at that time.

Friendship is a kind of power that, unlike allyship, does not rely on existing systems of privilege. In this world, that qualifies friendship as both a spiritual practice and superpower. The essential difference is this: To become an ally is to take on an identity. To become a friend is to commit to a path of practice. Friendship is not an identity—it's an activity. Friends feed each other, check in on each other, cheer each other up, and let each other be. We help when help is needed and wanted. We do our very best to protect each other from harm. We support each other in accountability when we fail to live up to our values and agreements. We begin again. Friendship is something we practice not because we should but because we want to. Because it restores our access to our full humanity. Because it makes life beautiful and meaningful and divine.

Fortunately, science has also begun to articulate just how amazingly necessary friendship actually is. Loneliness has been referred to as a global health epidemic by several world governments and found to decrease life expectancy more than anxiety, depression, or smoking fifteen cigarettes a day.[9] Leading researchers have also shown that chronic loneliness both increases the body's inflammatory response and decreases the immune system's ability to fight infection.[10] The absence of meaningful connections with other human beings is literally making us sick.

When friendships are weak, the impact isn't limited to our personal health. Families, communities, and even social movements become more vulnerable to outside stressors when friendships erode. Social movement facilitator Prentis Hemphill wrote an op-ed in the *Huffington Post* when they were the healing justice director at Black Lives Matter Global Network, highlighting the critical role of friendships in the day-to-day, moment-to-moment process of working together toward a more liberated future. "How we protect and care for each other along the way [to liberation], how we come through connected and stronger at the other end, are possibly the most critical and meaningful questions we face."[11] The violence that marginalized and targeted communities experience coming from external sources means that, within our communities, our friendships are an especially important, potentially life-saving force of safety, comfort, and care.

We are lucky to be living in a time when the value of friendship, both personal and political, is alive in our awareness. If it were easy, if knowledge alone was enough to instantly transform us into better friends, chances are we would all just do it. But it's not easy, especially when we add all our cultural conditioning, personal experiences, and personality quirks into the mix. There are so many reasons *why* we should prioritize friendship in this world. I see the *Mitta Sutta* as a set of directions that can support us in learning *how*. And, because we live in a world where industries, institutions, and political regimes benefit when we hate ourselves and disconnect from each other, we need all the support and direction we can get.

In our personal practices of radical friendship, we must make our minds environments where it is *safe to fail*. When part of the mind is always judging us, we are living inside a sense of self that is *never* good enough. The voice of oppression is fragmenting, whether it comes from outside us or inside our minds. It tells us that parts of us are undesirable, that we should create an inner distance from them, hide them from even our own view. In the practice of meditation, we have all these opportunities to welcome all of who we are into awareness. When our minds wander, when we forget the instructions or lose our intentions for practice, we can notice these things from the perspective that, in the grand scheme of things, there is nothing wrong with us. Paradoxically, that's the perspective that makes it possible for us to learn, grow, and change.

We must also cultivate inner environments where it is *safe to feel*. Inner separation hurts. For me, this is a primarily somatic practice. I feel the ache of the rift and the desire to no longer be at war with myself. Feeling it doesn't mean it will go away immediately. Turning toward feeling often makes uncomfortable sensations even more intense, at least at first. But, feeling is the first step on a path that will allow our inner landscapes to start to move and mend in the healing light of our own awareness. When meditating, I often imagine I am feeling the breaths of my dearest friend, each of them sustaining her life. *Precious*. I will even put my hand on my own heart and feel my chest move. *Worthy*. In this way, our minds become places where we are not only safe to feel suffering but also safe to feel completely loved and completely free.

The activities of radical friendship spring from an attitude of mind, a way of seeing what's true in the world and responding to it. I'll end this chapter with meditation because it is, in my experience, a super effective way to build up these inner capacities. When we make friends with ourselves—when we spend time doing the things that bring us well-being and pleasure and delight, when we tell ourselves that whoever and however we are is not only OK but also totally lovely—we become the kind of people others want to be around too. Our radical friendship is like a magnet. Changing ourselves doesn't automatically change the world, but it's an excellent place to start.

PRACTICE

Making Friends with Yourself

If you want to try this practice, start by finding a position for your body that is as comfortable as possible—it could be sitting in a chair or on a meditation cushion, lying down, or even standing up. Set a timer for an amount of time that works for you—it is totally OK to start with a few minutes and build up over time.

Close your eyes or lower them to the space in front of you. Softening the eyes can awaken your other senses, especially those of hearing and bodily sensation.

Begin with a gentle check-in. How is your mind doing right now? How's your heart? Your body? As you pause and feel into these different domains of your being, take the attitude that there is absolutely no part of you that needs to be pushed away. In truth, you're not actually fixing anything with meditation. You're just allowing some time and space for mind, heart, and body to catch up with each other, creating conditions that promote wholeness and healing.

As long as we are alive, thoughts, emotions, and bodily sensations will occur—often, all at the same time. In this meditation practice, we'll be using bodily sensations as a home base for our awareness, as a resting place for our attention to land. It's not that thoughts and emotions are unwelcome in any way—it's just that it's easier for the mind, heart, and body to synchronize when we bring our focus to one place at a time, and the body is for many of us an accessible, tangible place to rest our attention. Emotions and thoughts will come up, and when they do, you can just allow them to be there, dancing in the background, as you bring the experience of bodily sensation into the foreground of your attention.

We naturally pay attention to what we love. So, as you turn your awareness from your general check-in to paying closer attention to your body, try to do so with a sense of appreciation. Maybe you can even regard your body as your oldest, closest friend. It's been with you since the day you were born and will not ever leave you as long as you are alive. Whether you pay attention or not, it stays with you through all your waking and dreaming hours. And, when you do pay attention, your body receives that attention as a very basic form of love.

The language of the body is sensation. It speaks to us through pressure, relaxation, pulses, vibration, heat, coolness, tingles, prickles, and so on. As you survey the landscape of your body from within, see if you can find a place to rest your awareness—a place that feels neutral or pleasant. Some people love to pay attention to a place where they can feel the breath moving in the body—the nostrils, the chest, the belly—and let the changing sensations of breath be a soothing rhythm that lulls them into calm. Others prefer to focus on the feeling of lightness in the space behind their ears, or the grounding sensation of their hands or feet resting on something solid. Take the time you need to find a space in your body that works for you, and zoom in there slightly with your awareness; invite your attention to relax in that place, receiving the sensations of your body there and noticing when sensations change.

Allow the feeling and movement of each breath or other bodily sensation to be lit up by your awareness. No need to struggle with other aspects of your experience that will inevitably call your attention away. Your task is to periodically call your attention back to feeling the sensations that are arising in the location you've committed to for this brief period. Allow your awareness to stabilize and rest on the felt experience of your body in a way that feels pleasant or at least neutral.

From time to time, in the flow of thoughts, emotions, and other bodily sensations, you may suddenly realize that you've lost track of the sense of your body. It can even make you feel a little disoriented or panicky, like that feeling of losing your friends in a crowd—one moment, you think you're right there with them, and the next moment, they're nowhere to be found.

In this practice, you have only to return your awareness to your home base in your body again and—bam! In that instant, you're reunited. Every time you find yourself at home in your body again, let it be a moment of appreciation and celebration.

When your timer goes off or you decide to close the practice, take a few moments to reflect on the benefits of making friends with yourself and allowing your body to be a platform for establishing that relationship.

If you like, you may connect with the wish that everyone, everywhere, will truly make friends with their minds, hearts, and bodies in this lifetime.

Imagine what a world that would be.

(2)

Give What Is Hard to Give

> Monks, a friend endowed with [this]
> quality is worth associating with. . . .
> They give what is hard to give.
>
> —*Mitta Sutta*

WHEN THE BUDDHA took on new students, the very first practice he taught—before he taught meditation—was the practice of giving. Of the benefits of generosity, he said this:

> If beings knew, as I know, the results of giving and sharing, they would not eat without having given, nor would the stain of selfishness overcome their minds. Even if it were their last bite, their last mouthful, they would not eat without having shared, if there were someone to receive their gift.[12]

I love that, in these passages, the Buddha doesn't just suggest giving away our excess, the stuff that we don't really want and were going to get rid of anyway. He asks us to give what is actually a little difficult for us to part with,

41

because to hold back what we *could* otherwise share is to curb our enjoyment and tighten our hearts.

Radical friendship makes a practice of giving from the place where it stretches us just a bit beyond our comfort zone. That sensation of stretch we may feel in the practice of generosity happens because whenever we give, we are always also giving something up. In radical friendship, we are giving up something of lesser value to receive something of greater value—for example, giving up material goods or other resources to be of service to the people we care about. And through doing so, we get to liberate ourselves from the tendency of the mind to cling in ways that ultimately cause suffering for ourselves and everyone else.

What is hard to give will be different for each of us. So, for this chapter, I'm going to share my own big three acts of giving: time, material resources, and love in the form of unconditional friendliness. You may relate to them too, but even if you don't, I hope they inspire you to reflect on what you would be willing to give, or give up, to be a more radical friend.

GIVING TIME

My biggest teacher about the giving of time has been my bonus kid, Purple. When my partner and I moved to Philadelphia a few years back, his eight-year-old daughter started living with us every other week. I'd taught yoga and meditation to children in New York City public schools for over a decade, but I hadn't lived in the same house with a child since I was a kid myself. I just assumed my classroom management skills would be transferable to my new role as a coparent.

As a schoolteacher, I'd become pretty artful at managing time, designing lessons that took precisely forty-seven minutes—the exact length of our class periods. It took me a little while to understand that when getting from point A to point B, Purple time is about twice as long as my time.

Take, for example, the first time I walked Purple to school. School started at 8:15 a.m. I knew it took me ten minutes to walk there from our house. But, I didn't factor in the time it would take Purple to put on her shoes and realize that the ankle socks she was wearing made her feet feel weird inside her high-tops. Or, that the only other clean socks she had were these knee-high white ones that her dad bought her, which she said made her look like she was in a Harry Potter movie. Or, that at 8:05, I would still be digging through the hamper, trying to find socks that were neither *too* dirty nor made Purple's feet feel weird. I didn't realize that new flowers would have started blooming since the last time she walked to school this way and that at 8:10, she'd want to stop and tell me the names of the ones she knew and make up names for the ones she didn't.

I was getting agitated by the time we reached a path that I remembered we could take as a shortcut. Purple declared that I had to guess the password to open the invisible secret door first. We now had two minutes until the school day began—we could still make it if we hurried. I grunted and ignored her, walking right through her invisible door and speeding toward the school. When I looked back to see if Purple was following me, I saw her still standing there at the threshold, eyes wide as if I'd just broken something precious.

In that moment, I realized what had been driving me to rush. I had at some point decided that if we arrived on time, I was a good stepmom, and if we arrived late, I was a complete failure. As a new parent, I didn't really know what I was doing, and I didn't want the other parents or the teacher to know that. But the look of disappointment on Purple's face woke me right up from my fears of being judged. Getting her to school on time was important, and I would eventually get better at it. But the most important thing was building a relationship where we had enough time to imagine and play and dream together.

I turned back and retraced my steps. "OK, OK," I said. "I do know the password. It's . . . *tickle!*" I held up my hands, made wiggly fingers, and took one step toward her with an open-mouthed grin. She bolted down the walkway toward her school, screaming and laughing, and I jogged after her.

We arrived a few minutes late, but we made it.

When I read the Buddha's statement that the radical friend "gives what is hard to give," my first thought is of time. Time is my scarcest resource, the one I am most hesitant to give to other people, and even to myself. In an age of hypercapitalism, where time is money, slowing down feels like a luxury only the rich can afford.

Children, who often move a little slower than we adults do, give us a great gift in this rapidly accelerating world. Sensitivity, curiosity, and play can transform ordinary activities into extraordinary ones—and they all take time. If we're not willing to give time to be fully present for the needs of our friends, we start to see every unexpected event as an obstacle and we miss the ways that these events are also ordinary miracles when given the time to unfold.

On a good day, I know that the pace of real friendships— friendships that challenge hierarchy and connect us with what's really important in this life—is always slower than we think. All people have their own rhythm, and if we listen well, we can hear it. One activity of radical friendship is attuning to the cadence of our beloved others and shifting our own rhythms to move with theirs. I love the way the disability justice organizer Mia Mingus writes about this in a piece called "Wherever You Are Is Where I Want to Be: Crip Solidarity." Sharing her experience of being a disabled person in relationships with other disabled people, she writes to her beloved community: "I want to be with you. If you can't go, then I don't want to go. If we are traveling together, sharing political space together, building political family together, then I want to be with you. I want us to be together . . . We resist ableism dividing us."[13]

Pace is political. Giving each other the gift of time is a way of embodying freedom, moment by present moment.

This includes, of course, the time we give ourselves. It's so hard to give ourselves time when we feel like we don't *have* it. Pretty much everyone I know is working too much. Katie Loncke, co-director of the Buddhist Peace Fellowship, once called overworking "the smoking of our generation." Everyone is doing it, and we don't yet know the full scope of the consequences, but we are beginning to understand that it's even more dangerous than we thought.

Sometimes it's true that we can't afford to rest. And sometimes, we can't afford not to. Radical friendship with ourselves means we consider the time that we care for our bodies, minds, and hearts as a way to disrupt cultures of harm. Like the start-up–inspired "hustle culture" that glorifies nonstop work for the greatest possible financial reward. Or the burnout culture of so many nonprofit organizations, where activists, organizers, and direct service providers work themselves sick, responding to urgent crises around the clock.

I know that for me, and probably generations of my family lineage, burnout didn't always look like complete collapse. Burnout looked like continuing to work—in fact, working all the time—and finding that work sucked the enjoyment out of everything else. Working at maximum intensity over long periods not only frays our well-being but it also stresses our relationships and diminishes our creative capacity to do our capital "W" Work in the world.

The Buddhist teacher Mushim Ikeda wrote a vow that her students must commit to before they enter her year-long mindful activism program.

The vow goes like this:

Aware of suffering and injustice, I [name], am working to create a more just, peaceful, and sustainable world. I promise, for the benefit of all, to practice self-care, mindfulness, healing, and joy. I vow to not burn out.[14]

If we are already doing a lot of work to care for other people, this vow not to burn out by giving time, as Ikeda writes, "to practice self-care, mindfulness, healing, and joy" may be mostly aspirational. We may have to mutter it from the depths of overwork, in the middle of feeling we have nothing left to give anyway. If so, a vow like this can be a reminder to pull back from our hardened edges and into our soft centers. That center is where we can find the confidence that giving time where it's needed, including to ourselves, is actually a huge part of justice, peace, and sustainability work.

Another reason why Mushim's vow to not burn out is so genius is that the *fear* of burning out keeps a lot of people from becoming socially or politically engaged in the first place, or from reengaging if they've had to step away. There can be this feeling that the needs of the world are so great they will swallow us whole, so we keep our distance—caring, but not getting directly involved. A vow like the one Mushim offers her students, which includes both the commitment to work for justice *and* the commitment not to burn out by doing so, can provide a sense of balance. We can feel confident in engaging in activities that promote justice and interrupt harm—the essence of radical friendship. And, we can do so knowing that when we get overwhelmed, we will give ourselves the time to take refuge in practices that restore our energy and joy.

I suppose I should mention here that Buddhist vows are *notoriously* impossible to fulfill. The figure of the bodhisattva, prominent within the Mahayana Buddhist teachings, is an enlightened being who takes a vow not to transcend the earthly plane until every sentient being is also fully liberated. Their vow is wild, paradigm-shifting, and completely visionary. It's a promise to try something they may never achieve, and a promise to never to stop trying. To give time to ourselves and our loved ones for work, play, rest, spiritual practice, activism, art, and healing, all in a world where time is a scarce and precious resource—we will probably spend our whole lives calibrating the balance. Even if we never get it right, there is value in vowing to try. Trying, falling short, and trying again are all part of the journey. Radical friendship is a process of incremental change that, in the end, adds up to everything that counts.

GIVING MONEY

I recently read a study showing that with current rates of economic growth, it would take the average Black family 228 years to achieve the wealth of the average white family, and it would take the average Latinx family 84 years to do the same.[15] These inequalities are deeply rooted in historical injustices—colonization, enslavement, Jim Crow laws, and legal obstructions to ownership of land and property, to name just a few. And they continue to ripple through our present-day lives in policies like mass incarceration, defunding of public schools, and police harassment and brutality.

How can we even begin to quantify what was taken, the lives, land, languages, and cultures lost by way of colonization and enslavement? It's an equation that is downright overwhelming in scope. As friends, "giving what is hard to give" when it comes to our material resources means a radical shift in perspective. There's something revolutionary about giving money, land, and other resources to the people and organizations we value and want to thrive. Because when we do, we are taking the long view of history that makes it impossible to look at our resources and see them as our *possessions*. Any monetary wealth that ends up in our hands is the result of countless financial transactions. To be sure, not every one of them was a fair deal. In a moment of giving that involves a perceptual shift from "mine" to "ours," we help shift the culture of ownership and individualism that perpetuates economic injustice.

One of the most inspiring projects I know in the practice of giving as a radical friendship practice was set up by the Sogorea Te' Land Trust. Sogorea Te' is a women-led Indigenous community in the San Francisco Bay Area, founded with the intent to restore land parcels in urban areas to local Indigenous sovereignty. To fund this project, the community established a voluntary tax structure called the Shuumi Land Tax. The word *shuumi* means "to give" in the Indigenous language of the Karkin Ohlone people. The tax is a way that non-native people living in the Bay Area can give a specific amount of money, calculated on the value of their home, to fund the purchase of land that will then be stewarded by the descendants of the Chochenyo and Karkin Ohlone people, who were its original inhabitants.

When I asked Johnella LaRose, a cofounder of the trust, about the spiritual implications of the land tax, she talked about redistributing wealth as an activity that goes beyond charitable giving. In America, she said, land has gone from sacred space that is owned by no one, to public space owned by the US government, to private space owned by individuals and businesses. Now, she told me:

> We're trying to bring it back to the sacred. We're trying to bring it back to this place where everybody has access, safe places for people to be where they can relax and take a deep breath. We really feel like we have to look at the land as a relative, you know, and not as something, a real estate or property to be bought and sold.[16]

I like to think of the Shuumi Land Tax as one example of an experiment in popular reparations. It facilitates the rematriation of land into something more than a resource to be exchanged and, in the process, restores access to healing, sacred spaces for everyone to enjoy. When we learn the history of the land we live on, when we treat that land like a relative or friend, we notice its natural generosity, and our own gratitude overflows. When we're disconnected from the land, when we think of it as a thing, we take it for granted and damage it.

For many of us, the hardest thing about giving money from a rooted, spiritual place is that it's so hard to know how much is enough. The discomfort of uncertainty can lead us to give too much or too little, or to avoid giving all together because we just can't stand the internal debate. From the perspective of spiritual friendship, it's not just whether we give or how much that matters. The *spirit* with which we give is an essential element, whether we are making gifts between individuals, or from community to community.

There's another Buddhist teaching on generosity that can be wildly helpful in finding the spirit of generosity when we feel uncertain about whether and how much to give: the *Sappurisadana Sutta*.[17] It states that when giving is spiritual practice, the inner place from which we give has five particular qualities.

When we are in our integrity, it says, we give:

1. **"With a sense of conviction."** When the gift is right, we are sure. We may still feel a stretch, especially if the gift is big or giving is new. But there's no frenetic energy of debate around it—body and mind feel settled when we think of giving the right amount.

2. **"Attentively."** We bring our mindfulness with us before, during, and after the gift. When we give as radical friends—whether to individuals we know and love, to communities we care about and want to support, or even anonymously to people we don't know—it feels really, really good. Don't miss that feeling!

3. **"In season."** It's the right time—we have it to give, and the people to whom we're giving actually want what we have to offer.

4. **"With an empathetic heart."** So that we can feel, in a single moment, the joy of giving as well as receiving. Exchanges of generosity can be tender, full of vulnerability. When we give with a sense of our own full humanity and the full humanity of the person or people we're giving to, we resist objectifying each other and enrich each other's lives.

5. **"Without adversely affecting ourselves or others."** Some gifts come with a hook. Radical friends give within their means and without strings attached.

When giving money is done with awareness, honesty, and sensitivity, reallocating our financial resources opens us up. It opens us into a sense of gratitude for what we have, and a sense of responsibility for contributing what we can. It opens us into right relationship with one another and with the earth.

GIVING LOVE

Love is a spiritual resource. Unlike time and money, it isn't limited by material conditions. The capacity to love unconditionally is called *metta* in Pali and *maitri* in Sanskrit. Sometimes translated as "loving-kindness" or simply "friendliness," metta is a boundless state of heart and mind that everyone is born with. It is also a training in the practice of giving what is sometimes hard to give: unconditional friendliness as an unlimited resource.

So, what happens to us that makes love sometimes hard to give? How does as vast an energy as love become conditional?

Everybody I know has experienced some kind of hurt in a friendship. If we've survived primary school, we have surely felt unseen, unheard, rejected, or abandoned by someone we cared about and who we felt cared about us. Our hearts remember the pain of being caught off guard, the shame of feeling that we trusted unwisely. Not giving our love away so easily next time is a strategy for protecting our tender hearts in the future.

This strategy of self-protection can be even more prominent for those of us whose identities have been marginalized by society. If we have gotten the message not only from schoolmates but also from magazine covers, blockbuster movies, interactions with the legal system, and medical visits that we are undesirable, criminal, pathological, and disposable, well, we have every reason *not* to trust that the world at large has good intentions for us. The need to constantly assess whether others are going to use their power to hurt us is downright exhausting.

The metta practice offers us another kind of protection. It's not meant to do away with our well-earned reservations about trusting individuals and systems that have proved themselves to be w. Our hearts are made both to open and to close when needed. The metta practice is another skill to be added to our toolkit, a way of restoring the sense of an unbounded heart, and a support for its gradual expansion in alignment with our intentions. In his best-selling book *The*

Road Less Traveled, author and psychiatrist M. Scott Peck defined love as "the willingness to extend oneself for the purposes of our own or another's spiritual growth."[18] This quality of *extending* is the hallmark of metta. Unconditional friendliness wants to spread out; it desires expansion. When our hearts are full of this kind of love, we are emboldened to stretch, with wisdom, beyond our comfort zones. In doing so, we experience our true nature.

The first time the Buddha described metta, he taught it as an antidote to fear. In the story, the Buddha had advised a group of practitioners to go into the forest to meditate. They wandered and wandered and eventually encountered what looked like the perfect place: an undiscovered grove. They couldn't believe their luck! It was close enough to town that they could easily go there to find food, but far enough away that they wouldn't hear too much of the city hustle. It was by a stream with fresh water for drinking. They couldn't believe that no one already lived there.

The travelers settled in for the night, each of them going up into a different tree branch to sleep. But, soon they were awakened by a thousand angry tree spirits. "You've trespassed in our homes!" they screamed. "You've trampled our gardens! You've terrified our children!" The monks' hearts filled with fear and their minds were tormented with horrific, paranoid dreams all through the night. They became sick, saw threatening visions, and in the morning, they ran as fast as they could back to where the Buddha was staying. They told him all about the horrors of their harrowing night in the grove and pleaded with him not to send them back.

The Buddha told the fearful monks they *had* to go back. When they asked for weapons, he told them he would give them a much more effective form of protection. He taught them how to radiate unconditional friendliness to all beings, without exception or discrimination. And, he told them to infuse this generous form of love into their every thought, word, and action as they returned to the forest, newcomers in an already-occupied land.

In the Metta Sutta, the Buddha instructs:

Even as a mother protects with her life
Her child, her only child,
So with a boundless heart
Should one cherish all living beings:
Radiating kindness over the entire world:
Spreading upwards to the skies,
And downwards to the depths;
Outwards and unbounded
Freed from hatred and ill-will.
Whether standing or walking, seated or lying down
Free from drowsiness,
One should sustain this recollection.[19]

The way this story is normally told is that after the Buddha taught the monks loving-kindness, they returned to the grove, the evil tree spirits left them alone, and they got enlightened. *The end.* My personal experience with metta practice tells me that if these monks were really working it, they came back to the forest in a radically different way than they had entered it the night before. They asked for consent. They took cues from the forest spirits about where to settle, and once they did, they always regarded their neighbors' well-being as equal to their own. While it probably took some time to build trust with the tree spirits again after their reckless and inconsiderate behavior, I imagine that the monks and nuns who were now practicing metta remained humble, rigorous, and generous. They led with friendliness in their attitudes and all their actions, and the forest spirits responded with kindness too. Eventually, I imagine they reached a kind of social harmony that made their collective enlightenment possible.

We don't have the story as told from the perspective of the tree spirits. We can imagine, though, how it must be to have hundreds of people move all at once into your neighborhood, strain your resources, and demand you accommodate them. Having lived in major cities all my life and watched them transform under my feet, I can't help but read this as a gentrification story. How often have I heard new residents of a historical community exclaim while in line at a coffee shop how amazing it is that "no one lives here?" It's a settler-colonial mindset for the modern age. And, while the real villains in the hypergentrification of our cities are the real estate developers fishing for deals and the local government officials who fail to protect the people they are supposed to serve, each of us must also take personal responsibility for where we move and how we enter in.

However you read it, the origin of metta is a story for our times, because unconditional friendliness is a protection spell so fierce that it works in two directions. It protects others from the suffering we'd cause them if we were acting without it. And, it also protects each of us from the guilt and shame we'd feel when we realized we'd caused suffering without knowing it.

We can think of metta in its simplest form as the complete absence of hatred and fear. Hatred provokes aggression. Fear provokes aggression. And, it seems to be the case that love provokes love. I've frequently had encounters with whole groups of people who seem irritated by my very presence and are poised to struggle with me. It happens most often when I'm in a position of authority—teaching, facilitating, leading in some way—among people who have greater privilege than I do in society at large. Energetically, it's like being in a tug-of-war.

When I'm able to generate the wish that whoever is holding the other end of the rope experiences happiness, health, and freedom, when I'm able to give them this essential form of love, something changes. I soften, they soften, and sometimes we find a way to meet each other again, freshly disarmed. This wish doesn't mean that I just stand there and let them harm me. It just means that I'm sending out a strong signal that I have no intention of harming *them*. When I'm able to center the intention to do no harm—even in the midst of fear or defensiveness (my own or other people's)—it brings me a deep sense of peace.

With love, as with money and time, our practice of generosity is at its most radical when we give it with wisdom. Am I suggesting that you become best friends with everyone, no matter what they say or do? Absolutely not. But, I *am* suggesting that there may be more love available to each of us in this world than we are currently experiencing, and that there may be more love inside you than you currently have avenues with which to express it. We can all grow our capacity to give and receive the love we need. The practice of radical friendship is one of building a bigger container for that love, with a healthy dose of wisdom about how, when, and to whom we give it.

PRACTICE

Metta Meditation

To cultivate the heart of metta, of unconditional friendliness, we begin with ourselves—picturing ourselves as if from the outside, either as we are now or at a moment in our lives when we radiated goodness and love. If it feels more easeful, you can even conjure an image of yourself from your childhood, a photo where the essence of your beautiful, innocent spirit just shines. Once you have the image in mind, remind yourself silently of all the ways you have been courageous, kind, patient, honest, and otherwise fantastic in this lifetime. Sometimes when people do this, they find that what comes to mind instead is all the times when they were kind of shitty. We can think of this as a purification, where the force of love is shaking loose everything that blocks love. Those blockages rise to the surface of the mind to be released. It's helpful to periodically relax our bodies as we meditate and to keep breathing.

As you train your inner vision on yourself and your innate loveliness, silently offer yourself the following phrases:

> *May I be safe and protected from inner and*
>   *outer harm.*
> *May I be happy and peaceful in body, heart,*
>   *and mind.*
> *May I be as healthy and strong as can be.*
> *May I live with ease.*
> *May I give and receive all the love that I need.*
> *May I feel that love right now.*[20]

In this practice, you use these phrases as the object of concentration, the home base for your attention to return to when it wanders—just like you did when you returned to the sensations of your body in the last meditation. As you repeat these phrases to yourself several times, slowly, notice what it feels like to give yourself these loving wishes and what it feels like to receive them.

After spending a few minutes giving these loving wishes to yourself, you can continue the practice by visualizing specific people and groups of people and imagining yourself giving the same phrases to them. This is a way of embodying the expanding, generous quality of metta.

Start with a person to whom it is easy for you to give love—a hero, a benefactor, someone who has inspired or advocated for you. Picture that person in as much detail as possible. Feel what it's like to be in their presence. Imagine how their eyes would crinkle with love when they see you. In your mind's eye, try to see yourself offering them the metta phrases, like a beam of light from your heart to theirs:

May you be safe and protected from inner and
  outer harm.
May you be happy and peaceful in body, heart,
  and mind.
May you be as healthy and strong as can be.
May you live with ease.
May you give and receive all the love that you need.
May you feel that love right now.

After repeating all the phrases a few times and seeing this being receive and integrate your good wishes, you can wave goodbye to them for now and allow their image to dissolve.

Extending your love to a friend is the next step in the practice. Picture a friend in your mind's eye, the first person you think of when you contemplate that word—someone you love and want the best for, even though your relationship isn't always perfect. Know that with friends, it is common to feel a subtle sense of demand under our love. We wish our friends health—and we *really* wish they would take our advice about diet and exercise. Or, we wish our friends could live with ease—so they would stop complaining already about being so stressed out. It's love with a hook, and while it's certainly not the same as wishing someone harm, our mixed intentions are not as free as they could be. When we notice a feeling of "push" when we give love to someone, we can only do our best to internally take a step back and offer our wish again, this time without strings attached. Center your friend's image in your mind's eye, bring forth the good in them with your inner loving gaze, and offer them the same phrases you offered to yourself and your hero. Notice what it feels like to give those phrases and to see your friend receive them.

Next you can bring to mind a person who is neutral to you. This is someone you might see regularly, but who you don't know very well, and toward whom you don't have a particularly positive or negative feeling. A lot of students I've worked with choose someone who provides a service for them—the person who delivers their mail, makes their latte, does their dry cleaning, or performs other service roles. Before you offer the phrases to this familiar stranger, consider their full life, beyond their role in your routine. This is undoubtedly someone who loves and is loved by others, who has known joy and sorrow, gain and loss. Someone who, like all of us, just wants to be happy and not suffer.

Giving love to people we don't know is a tipping point in our capacity for spiritual friendship at the collective level. We don't have to know someone personally to care about, honor, and bless their lives. And so, as you picture your neutral person, picture yourself sending them the same wishes from your heart to theirs. Recognize that you may often be extending love across a difference in class or culture, across the imaginary line dividing the known from the unknown.

Notice what it feels like to give unconditional friendliness and keep giving, repeating the phrases for some time.

The next instruction is to bring to mind someone to whom it is actually a little difficult for you to give friendly wishes. Not your *most* difficult person—just someone who is kind of annoying or irritating in some way. Here, too, try to see the person's full humanity and to look with compassionate eyes at their attempts to be happy, however backward or ill-advised they may be. Maybe if they were actually happy and peaceful, they wouldn't be so irritating. So, as best you can, picture them and offer them the metta phrases with a warm heart. If need be, you can imagine the difficult person as a baby, totally innocent, completely sensitive, and clearly full of goodness. When we have a hard time with someone, we tend to objectify them in our minds, flatten them so that we only see them one way. Our goal is to stretch our hearts by shifting our internal relationship with them, imagining the lovability within them that we don't usually see. It doesn't mean we let them treat us any way they want. True love for ourselves wouldn't allow it. But, it does mean we don't cancel the person out of our hearts. We don't have to like someone to love them.

The most generous heart we can aspire to grow is one that is able to love all beings—whether or not we know them, like them, or share identities or experiences or views. We finish the metta practice by inviting all beings everywhere into our minds for a few moments—as far as our awareness can stretch. Those that walk on the land, swim in the water, fly through the air, and crawl through the earth.

From single-celled organisms to the tallest redwood tree. At this point, we turn metta into "we" phrases, opening our hearts to ourselves and everyone else with equal regard:

May we all be safe and protected from inner and
　　outer harm.
May we all be happy and peaceful in body, heart,
　　and mind.
May we all be as healthy and strong as can be.
May we all live with ease.
May we all give and receive all the love that we need.
May we all feel that love right now.

With this, we may feel the tenderness of how living beings have different needs that sometimes conflict with one another. Our minds may wrestle with how, in nature, life for one being may mean death for another. In this practice, we get to see what it's like to wildly wish that all beings, without exception, be completely well and to extend our wishes to all of them equally, even when we can't control their experience. In this way, we become a love machine, spreading our highest wishes in all directions. The capacity to give unconditional friendliness is something we're born with, and in an unjust world, it sometimes gets harder to give along the way. The idea with metta is that when we practice giving what is hard to give, it eventually gets easier. Like water over rock, it will eventually wash away the obstacles to giving love and open the channels to receiving love in return.

(3)

Do What Is Hard to Do

Monks, a friend endowed with [this]
quality is worth associating with . . .
They do what is hard to do.

—*Mitta Sutta*

TRULY RADICAL FRIENDSHIPS require our wholehearted
effort. I believe this is a fact, but to be honest, it's not always one I want to hear. And it's not because I'm lazy. It's
because I'm already doing so many things that are hard to.
Work, family, partnership, politics—all of these relationships can be such a struggle. So my spirit groans a little
when I think of friendship as yet another space where I'm
called to do things that are hard. I want my friendships to
be easy, pleasurable, and low-key. And I've been tempted to
argue that if friendships require me to do more than what
living in an unjust world already requires, then maybe they
just aren't worth it. Maybe you can relate.

Where did I get this idea, that friendship should be easy?
Was it the buddy movies of the eighties that taught me that
friendship means a trusty sidekick to my main character,

one who would always be there to support and defend me? Could it have been the BFF necklaces I used to run my fingers over at shopping mall booths back in middle school? Those heart pendants that split into two pieces, each half on its own chain for each one of the Best Friends Forever to wear around their necks. Forever. I had friends, of course, but did I have a *Best Friend Forever?* Forever seemed like an impossibly long time. Perhaps the sense that friendship should be easy was solidified for me on social media. When scrolling through snapshots of friends with open mouthed grins chatting over lattes, I often imagine their relationships as one big, leisurely, well-lit coffee date. Which, of course, they are not. They can't be. I know, because I've posted pics like that of myself with friends who, weeks or months later, are stressing me out.

I do think there are some friendships that run just fine on autopilot. But I don't think there are many of those that would qualify as radical, spiritual friendships. Because when we're approaching our relationships as a spiritual path and we give our whole hearts, we're also exposing ourselves to hurt. In the safety of dedicated friendship, all kinds of relational wounds make themselves known, sometimes seemingly brought on by the slightest provocation. Just as in deep meditation, our old stuff can come up to the surface. Only, when it happens in friendship, usually the other person knows it too. In more superficial relationships, that's the end of the story. In radical friendship, it's just the beginning.

The Buddha proposed that the spiritual friend is someone willing to "do what is hard to do." And when it comes to friendship, perhaps one of the hardest things to do is to acknowledge that these relationships aren't always easy. Sure, there's plenty of joy and hilarity and fun to be had in friendship, but friends can also break your heart. Of course, from the Buddhist perspective, that's not necessarily always a bad thing. It just means that there's work to be done.

The nature of that work, the energy of it, matters just as much as the work itself. On this path of practice, *how* we effort is every bit as important as where and why we apply that effort. Have you ever used a power drill to do a job better suited for a good, old-fashioned screwdriver? I have, and let me tell you, the wood was not pleased. Friendships take some work, but they don't require our maximum effort all the time. Using too much juice as we reflect on and engage in our radical friendship work can leave us, and our friends, feeling bulldozed. Too little effort though, and it's not enough to make an impact. We kind of float through, bypassing all kinds of opportunities to grow in wisdom and understanding and love. Wise effort is finding the just-right amount of energy to attend to our hearts when they hurt and to assess the root cause of that hurt. It's also the effort needed to imagine ourselves into a more liberated way of showing up and dedicating ourselves to practicing that way of being in all areas of our lives.

So yes, radical friendship can be hard work, but that doesn't mean it has to be a burden. It's work that results in a certain kind of happiness, one that the Buddha referred to as the "joy of blamelessness." It's the joy that comes from living in integrity with our values. It's the happiness that arises when we break a sweat in the beautiful struggle, that feeling of having carried on with our purpose even when confronted with a huge obstacle. The hard work of radical friendship is like the daily effort to brush our teeth. We may not always feel like it, but we come to love the minty-fresh feeling in our spirits so much that the effort is worth the reward. It's the kind of hard work that brings more ease, peace, and freedom in the end, and radical friendship is worth it.

FOUR NOBLE TRUTHS AS A METAPHOR FOR HEALING

One of the things I love about the Buddhist approach to liberation is that it's rooted in a deep experiential understanding of cause and effect. The view is that if we do the hard work of understanding the ways we get caught, in our friendships or anywhere else in our lives, then we can have insight into how we get free.

The blueprint for exploring this view is a framework called the Four Noble Truths, and it is sometimes described through a metaphor of healing. Suffering is the illness, and the path to liberation is the remedy. The first noble truth is the diagnosis—the observable signs of dis-ease, whether in the individual body, heart, and mind, or within society at large. The second noble truth states that the underlying cause of suffering can always be traced back to a clinging of some kind. The third and fourth noble truths offer a solution, assuring us that healing is possible and prescribing a path that brings us back to health.

These truths are known as noble because they describe universal features of every human experience. There is no one on this planet whose life is only suffering, with not a single moment of freedom or joy. And likewise, there is no one who gets to have only joy, pleasure, and freedom and who never experiences suffering. In this way, our experience of both suffering and of liberation connects us to all of life, and there is a kind of nobility in this connection. The second reason these truths are noble is that when we recognize them and consciously work with them, we develop wisdom in a way that reveals our fundamental dignity. They provide a context that allows us to relate with reality rather than run from it, and we develop the skills we need to transform ourselves and our world.

First Noble Truth (the Diagnosis): Suffering

The Pali word for suffering is *dukkha*. It's a word that was historically used to describe the experience of being in a vehicle with unevenly shaped wheels that made for a bumpy ride. Dukkha can refer to a whole range of uncomfortable states, all the way from a little stress or mild discomfort to the most abject pain or profound grief. This first noble truth calls us to recognize that even if much of our human experience is beautiful, there will always be stress of some kind too. This truth names part of the experience of being alive, the poignant bittersweetness of both the ubiquity of struggle and the fact that we're never alone in it. It is the end of denying the way things are.

Being real can be a healing practice in its own right. How

many of us grew up in homes where we were not supposed to acknowledge things that were clearly going on right before our eyes? How many of us are grown now and still in the habit of pretending everything is fine, just *fine*? The problem with pretending is that eventually we will kind of believe ourselves, and then we will be truly confused. The first noble truth doesn't require that we call anybody in, or out, or do anything at all externally, not at first anyway. It simply asks us to notice, feel, and understand the truth of how things really are, *for us*, in our own experience.

As a radical friendship practice, we start the hard work of the noble truths by being real about the ways in which our friendships are imperfect. Because that's also dukkha—imperfection, unsatisfactoriness, ungraspability, and so on. In the Buddha's very first dharma talk called the Dhamma-cakkapavattana Sutta, or the "Setting Rolling the Wheel of Dharma" Sutta (I love that translation), he defined dukkha in the following categories:

- Birth, aging, and death
- Sorrow, lamentation, pain, grief, and despair
- Association with the unbeloved
- Separation from the loved
- Not getting what is wanted[21]

We can study all of these experiences in our friendships. I say "study" because the radical invitation of the first noble truth is to lean in and get intimate with situations that we may normally try to avoid. Of course, there's no need to go on an archeological dig—if we're not experiencing dukkha in friendship in any given moment, we can just relax and enjoy the ride. Nor is this an invitation to a pity party, where we mournfully catalogue every painful experience we've ever had and lick our wounds. It's more like a tool. When we do feel an "ouch" of some kind, we can bring our curious explorer-minds to the experience. What is the nature of this experience? Where exactly does it hurt?

IS IT LONELINESS? As I mentioned earlier, long before the COVID-19 pandemic, before we even imagined a global lockdown, the World Health Organization identified loneliness as a major health issue, especially in industrialized nations. Social isolation was a part of it, and it was observed even back then that many people were spending less time with their friends, family, neighbors, and coworkers. Factors like poverty, unemployment, major illness, decreased mobility, and abuse are known to exacerbate isolation, keeping people physically apart from the rest of the world for reasons beyond their control. One solution, social scientists tell us, is increasing the number of interactions we have with others, preferably in person, on a daily basis. Even small interactions like those we might have at the supermarket or bus stop significantly benefit health outcomes for those of us who are used to spending most of our time alone.

But the *feeling* of loneliness is a much more subjective measure than isolation. And while social isolation can contribute to loneliness, it's not the only cause. It's fairly common for people to feel disconnected, unwanted, and unloved, even with fully stacked social networks, even in a room full of people. Feeling lonely even when we're not actually alone has consequences just as dire as isolation, even physical ones—it's been shown that persistent feelings of loneliness can reduce our lifespans as much as smoking half a pack of cigarettes a day.[22]

Authenticity is an antidote to loneliness. I know that my own loneliest times were also the times when I felt the least safe to be fully me. Which makes sense, right? If we're shrinking, projecting, or performing—if we're not letting ourselves be known, it makes sense that we'd feel as if no one really knows us. Sometimes that impulse to not show up authentically is actually our wisdom talking. Not all spaces are safe spaces to express who we are inside. But knowing that doesn't make the loneliness less achy. Sometimes we are actually safe, but we just don't feel that way. Hiding inside of our friendships and the loneliness that follows can be habits, holdovers from an earlier time. We may know that and still have a hard time letting go. Double ouch.

However it shows up for us and whatever the causes, the first noble truth just asks us to notice and name it. *Loneliness.* Go ahead and put your hand on your heart. Take a deep breath.

IS IT DISAPPOINTMENT? Disappointment is the sadness we feel when we expected something better than we got. We were counting on a friend to show up, and they canceled. We hoped they would take our advice, and they took someone else's. We wanted them to know what we needed without having to say it, and they misread our cues. We got what we didn't want or we didn't get what we did want, and now we feel small and distant and tight.

To be clear: expectations themselves are not the enemy. Often the meaning we make of being disappointed is that we should have known better than to hope and dream, so we decide to live without any expectations at all. First of all—good luck with that. But also—we *should* expect to be treated with love, care, and respect from our friends. It's not only OK, it's good to have standards for how we want our friends to show up in a relationship. It's also natural to feel sad when someone doesn't live up to those standards.

What happens with disappointment though, is that we take other people's behavior as a measure of our personal worth. We think, if they didn't show up, then that must have something to do with us. We can take their actions as evidence for any pre-existing hurtful ideas that we have about ourselves—that we're unlikeable, not good enough, or unworthy of real friendship. Or we can take their actions as evidence for our ideas about the world at large—that no one can truly be trusted, that people only think about themselves, and so on. These thoughts are the mind's attempt at protecting us from future hurt by armoring up our hearts. If only that actually worked! Instead, thoughts like these usually add weight to the heart's already heavy load.

If in your disappointment you begin to believe that something is fundamentally wrong with you, or with people in general, you can practice with the first noble truth by taking a step back from whirling, defensive thinking. Don't let your thoughts add on to an already hurtful experience. Stay with the feeling for a while, giving it the attention and care it really needs. *Disappointment. Disappointment feels like this.* Put your hand on your belly, softly. Breathe.

IS IT COMPARING OR COMPETING? In my early twenties, one of my best friends was also a yoga instructor working in under-resourced communities in New York City. Like me, she was a Black woman who had natural hair and a bubbly spirit. But that was where the similarities ended, for the most part. We had different skin tones, body types, hair styles, and most importantly, our personalities and approaches to teaching were super distinct. We loved and respected each other in our similarities and in our differences. We cracked each other up and helped each other take ourselves less seriously. We inspired each other too—we got serious about Buddhist meditation around the same time and put each other on to retreats, workshops, and trainings we could take together, where we could build our skills and enjoy each other's company.

We also grew into more visible teaching and leadership positions around the same time. As we did, we found we were regularly being mistaken for each other at events where only one of us was present. Presenters treated us as interchangeable, booking one or the other of us, but never both at the same time. And because there weren't so many gigs for Black women yoga and meditation teachers at the time, a subtle sense of competition started to pervade our interactions whenever work came up in our conversations.

These experiences fueled my comparing mind. In Buddhism, the part of our mind that evaluates us in relationship to other people is called *manas*. It is literally translated as "conceit," and its function is to evaluate whether we are better than, lesser than, or the same as another person. It's a deeply rooted tendency in all of us, said to be one of the last bad habits to fall away as we approach enlightenment. Manas is always a source of suffering, but when it comes up in friendship it feels especially painful. It's hard to admit that we're having trouble wholeheartedly rooting for our friends because we're worried that their success will dull our shine.

As a first noble truth practice, when you notice comparing mind, redirect your attention from evaluating how your friend is doing and return it to your own heart. Get intimate with how it actually feels to compete with someone you love and the feelings of fear and scarcity that may be there too. Resist the shame of feeling like you *shouldn't feel this way*, just be with the feeling itself in a loving way. *Comparing feels like this.* Put a gentle hand on your cheek. Breathe deep.

IS IT CHANGING? Like all living things, friendships have a birth, aging, and death process. Or as we usually think about them, a beginning, a middle, and an end. When our friendships change in ways that we like, change feels like a good thing. Like a deepening relationship with someone we admire, a new level of honesty in an old friendship, or finally letting go of a relational pattern that no longer serves us—these are all deeply pleasant experiences. (Though it's said that if we look closely, even pleasant changes can be low-key stressful, because at some level we know things can change again.)

When friendships change in ways we *don't* like, the dukkha of change is more obvious. Maybe another relationship begins to take up more room in a friend's life, leaving less time and energy for us. Maybe we have an experience of someone that changes the way we feel about them. Maybe *we've* changed—our interests or values have shifted and as a result, an existing friendship is no longer a good fit. Ouch, ouch, and ouch.

The suffering of change in friendship is perhaps the aspect of suffering we have the least amount of control over. And in an effort to gain control, there can be a tendency to blame yourself or other people for what doesn't feel good in the face of change. For now, as a first noble truth practice, suspend your investigation of who's responsible and allow yourself to rest in the knowing that change is the way of the universe, and sometimes it just hurts. *This is change. Changing feels like this.* Feel the steadiness of the earth below you, supporting you even as things shift. Breathe.

MEET ALL SUFFERING WITH COMPASSION All suffering should be met with compassion. All of it. Whenever an open heart comes into contact with suffering, our own or someone else's, compassion is what automatically arises. Our job is to keep our heart open. We don't engage in the first noble truth, admitting when there's pain or stress in our relationship, as a way to beat ourselves up or reinforce the notion that we're somehow messed up and unworthy of love. We do it to connect more intimately with the reality of our common human experience so that we can open to it more tenderly. And in the metaphor of the four noble truths as a healing path, this knowing of dukkha with compassion is the way in to begin understanding its true roots.

Second Noble Truth (the Cause): Clinging

The Pali word *thanha* describes the cause of suffering. Often translated as "clinging," in Pali it means something like "thirst," which is really how many of us experience it—an unbearable discomfort and a longing for relief. Whenever we feel grabbed inside, when we feel rigidity take hold, when there's a sense of solidifying ourselves or objectifying others, we can be sure that thanha is present.

The second noble truth is an invitation to investigation. What is the actual cause of the suffering we are experiencing? How far down does the clinging start? If we just treat the symptoms, if we just attempt to alleviate the discomfort without understanding what causes it, we'll experience the same suffering over and over again. As healers of our own hearts, we want to get to the bottom of the underlying condition and heal it from the root.

The interesting thing about the suffering we experience in relationship is that it can have many roots, not just one. Often the most immediately apparent roots are those of our personal experiences, like how our early childhood, prior relationships, and the tendencies we were born with have shaped our habits and beliefs. Here, clinging shows up in our relationship with ourselves—limiting how we see and experience ourselves, and solidifying stories we tell ourselves about who we really are. It's also common to notice the clinging that arises in the interpersonal space, where our beliefs shape our interactions with other people. Here we may sense overgrown desires for companionship, approval, and validation, ones that exceed our basic human needs for love and connection. Or we may find the complete opposite—the desire to separate ourselves, to withdraw or disappear, in order to avoid the messiness of relationship and being hurt in it.

It's harder to see the roots of clinging where they exist in the systemic and societal realms. The ways they show up in our friendships can be less obvious than the way our personal and interpersonal conditioning does. But the policies and practices in our schools, workplaces, hospitals, and courts have had a profound impact on how we experience ourselves, each other, and the world as a whole. So too have societal forces like economic systems, religions, histories, and cultures.

Take, for example, the comparing mind I experienced in my relationship with my yoga teacher friend. As a personal experience, that moment in our relationship definitely touched on my own tendency to feel unseen and undervalued. As an interpersonal experience, it showed up as comparing mind with a side of judgment and competition. But how had the biases we'd experienced our whole lives as we interacted with other Black women in a racist society shaped our interactions? Would we have had the same kind of friction in our relationship had we not been constantly mistaken for each other in professional spaces? Or if there had been room for many Black women in leadership in our white dominated field instead of just a handful?

As radical friends, we must always ask the question: *does this suffering have a systemic root?* Systems of oppression tend to be *felt* as interpersonal experiences. There are ways we can mediate the impacts of those systems through how we relate to one another, and there's something incredibly healing about that. It can be just as healing to see how much relational stress comes not so much from our own clinging but from the persistent clinging of societal injustice in our lives.

We live in an interdependent universe. When we experience the suffering of oppression, it doesn't always necessarily mean that we are the ones who are clinging. Our lives are so deeply intertwined that clinging in one part of our social fabric can cause a snag to appear somewhere else. We can see this at a global scale in climate catastrophe, where the extraction of resources and toxic emissions in one area of the planet can cause deadly storms and drought somewhere else entirely. And in much the same way, we can feel systemic clinging in the form of injustice show up downstream in our friendships. The impacts of navigating biases, stereotypes, and prejudices in society our whole lives—the lack of trust along with feelings of unworthiness, loneliness, and disappointment—they can erode our capacity to connect and stay close in our friendships.

According to the Buddha, there *is* a way out of this cycle of clinging and suffering. And that's what the third noble truth is all about.

Third Noble Truth (the Prognosis): Freedom

"Freedom" and "liberation" are the most common translations for *nibbana*, the Pali word for the third noble truth (*nirvana* in Sanskrit). Etymologically, it means something like the extinguishing of a flame that has been burning. The term nibbana encourages us to think of liberation not as an experience of attaining something, but rather as an experience of letting go. In an analogy of the Buddha as a healer, the third noble truth is the metaphorical prognosis, and it is a hopeful one: complete healing, complete liberation, is actually possible for every one of us.

What would it feel like to be completely free? In its ultimate manifestation, nibbana is said to be the uprooting of all greed, hatred, and delusion. While it's an experience that is beyond language, there is a discourse in which the Buddha offers several synonyms that, taken together, can give us a sense of what nibbana might be like:

It is the Unformed, the Unconditioned, the End, the Truth, the Other Shore, the Subtle, the Everlasting, the Invisible, the Undiversified, Peace, the Deathless, the Blest, Safety, the Wonderful, the Marvellous, Nibbana, Purity, Freedom, the Island, the Refuge, the Beyond.[23]

In the everyday sense, we all have mini-nibbanas all the time. We find liberation when we forget to be self-conscious because we are so thoroughly in love with another human being. We encounter freedom when we go looking for an old resentment and find only forgiveness residing in that space. There is taste of nibbana in the sense of relaxation we feel when we have stopped grasping for what we want and have started wanting what we already have. When it comes to creating more freedom in our friendships, the liberation of the third noble truth is in the dreaming of and living into unburdened ways of being and relating. It's believing in our inherent capacity to let go of whatever is between us and real freedom.

In her short story "Evidence," the Black feminist scholar Alexis Pauline Gumbs imagines a liberated future after racialized capitalism. A future in which equity and justice are all we know, and violence and domination are distant memories. The story is written in a series of letters, the last of which is a letter of encouragement from Alexis's future self to her current one. She writes:

Dear Lexi,

Breathe deep, baby girl, we won. Now life, though not exactly easier, is life all the time. Not chopped down into billable minutes, not narrowed into excuses to hurt and forget each other. I am writing you from the future to remind you to act on your belief, to live your life as a tribute to our victory and not as a stifling reaction to the past. I am here with so many people you love and their children and we are eating together and we are tired from full days of working and loving but never too tired to remember where we come from. Never exhausted past passion and writing. So, I am writing you now . . .

Everybody eats. Everybody knows how to grow agriculturally, spiritually, physically, and intellectually. . . . We are more patient than we have ever been. And now that our time is divine and connected with everything, we have developed skills for how to recenter ourselves. We walk. We drink tea. We are still when we need to be. No one is impatient with someone else's stillness. No one feels guilty for sitting still. Everybody is always learning how to grow . . .[24]

This vision of liberation appears in a volume called *Octavia's Brood*. The collection is the outcome of a project in which coeditors adrienne maree brown and Walidah Imarisha asked social justice activists to write works of visionary fiction—something many of them had never done on paper before. However, as Imarisha later said in an interview about the project, change-makers are always writing compelling fictional futures to expand what we all think is possible.

Every time we imagine a world without borders, without prisons—that's science fiction. We have

never seen that world. But we can't build something we can't see. . . . We absolutely need fantastical
genres like science fiction, like fantasy, genres that
not only allow us to step beyond the boundaries
of what we are told is possible, but demand that
we do, demand that we engage our imaginations.
Because all real deep substantive social change has
been considered to be utterly unrealistic when it
happened. We need genres like these so that we can
learn to start not with the question 'What is a real-
istic change or win?' but with the question 'What
is the world we want to build?'"[25]

When it comes to envisioning the third noble truth
of liberation as it pertains to our collective future, sitting
with the question *What is the world that we want to build?* is
a wonderful place to begin. It requires a big stretch of our
imaginations to boldly dream into a future we have never
seen or known. And it is tremendously vulnerable too. How
many of us were laughed at as children, told we were na-
ive to dream of a world free from hatred and poverty and
war? How many of us learned in school that history is the
story of violence and domination, that human beings are
naturally self-centered, and that it is our destiny to continue living this way into the future? So, when we say we
imagine a world in which the earth and all its beings are
safe, protected, and loved, we are likely to come up against
our inner skeptic. Don't worry about that. Dream anyway.
Teach yourself to dream big again, to dream of liberated

relationships, and of a world that we all want to live in and are proud to pass on when we go.

Once you clarify that vision and concretely sense the elements and the feeling of the liberation that your heart desires, start to look around at your own mind and heart. Look at your relationships, organizations, and communities, and consider this question: *Where do I see the seeds of that liberation beginning to sprout right here and now?* Most of us default to noticing what is wrong or lacking in ourselves and our friendships. It's a tendency that can be valuable when it helps us know what we need to change, but in that default setting, we sometimes miss the bright spots, the areas of high potential, and the bits of evidence that the future we dream of is already germinating here in the present moment.

The third noble truth reminds us that freedom from suffering is possible. The artists within us and among us know how to make that vision of liberation visible so we can share it. The cause of that freedom, and the directions for how we nurture that freedom and how we actually embody the liberation we dream of, is described in the pathway of the fourth noble truth.

Fourth Noble Truth (the Prescription): The Path

The fourth noble truth, *magga*, states that there is a path we can follow that will lead us to the liberation we seek. Actually, there are many paths. The Buddha said there are eighty-four thousand dharma doors, each of them unique ways of opening to universal truth. These doorways can be found in wisdom traditions all over the world, in every culture. There is no such thing as the best path or right path for all people or for all of time. There is only the right path for *us*, right *now*.

The path of practice outlined in the fourth noble truth is called the Eightfold Path, and it offers us eight entry points into a process of liberation that integrates awareness, action, and reflection. It's a path that is always beginning from wherever we are right now, and it's divided into three main categories: wisdom, ethics, and meditation. I'm going to end this chapter with a brief description of each and a few examples about how each has contributed to my process of becoming a more radical friend. The path will look different for each one of us, but my hope here (and throughout this book) is that sharing my experience will help you to reflect on *your own* experience, and to navigate your own path to more liberated relationships.

WISDOM Wisdom isn't just intelligence or book-smarts—it's the deep knowing that comes from examining our lived experiences, being with the truths of our lives, and allowing that knowledge to shape our perceptions, intentions, and actions. Within the Eightfold Path, it is made up of two elements: wise view and wise intention.

Wise view means perceiving ourselves and each other through an understanding of cause and effect as described in the four noble truths. It means seeing clearly when there is suffering in our relationships and being willing to name it. It also means looking deeply for the true cause of that suffering, whether it is our own attachments and aversions that are causing us pain or those of our friend, the changing nature of relationships, or the clinging of the wider systems we have been shaped by and must contend with. With wise view, we see the pain points in our relationships not as the truth of who we are, nor necessarily even our fault, but rather opportunities to see where we still have room to grow, individually and collectively. And of course, the wise view never loses sight of freedom—in this case, the vision of friendships that are deconditioned from oppressive belief systems, free from the endless cycles of too much and not enough. Wise view sees relationships in which we feel loved and safe and whole exactly as we are, and it has confidence that the seeds we plant of liberated friendships will always sprout given the right conditions. The existence of both suffering and liberation in all of our relationships is hard for the conventional mind to perceive, but for our wisdom eyes it's no problem. The wise heart is spacious enough to hold the *both/and* of our friendships, in all their complexities and contradictions.

The second element of wisdom, **wise intention**, means being crystal clear about what we value and allowing those values to guide us on a day-to-day, moment-to-moment basis. If we have a goal destination in mind, then our intention is our navigation system for getting there. If our intent is to show up for our own and each other's liberation, and to be in relationship with people who show up for us, we must ask ourselves: *what are the qualities of heart and mind that can keep us headed in that direction?* If you'd like to work with wise intention, you may even start with one of the characteristics of spiritual friendship outlined in the *Mitta Sutta*—generosity, wise effort, endurance, honesty, etc.—and choose to work with it for a little while. In moments of confusion or indecision, you can ask yourself, *What would be the most generous thing to do in this moment?* Your intention can point you toward your next right move.

ETHICS The second pillar of teachings in the eightfold path is about how we live our values, how we take our clarity, understanding, and highest intentions and practice them in everyday interactions. It's composed of three elements: wise speech, actions, and livelihood.

Wise speech is the practice of bringing our inner world out into the world around us, to share our views and intentions with other people. This bridge between our inner and outer life can happen through vocal speech, or any number of other modes of expression. Emailing, tweeting, and posting all fall under this domain. Our world is a noisy one, and communication moves fast—sometimes faster than the speed of our practice. The Buddha's teachings offer several guidelines for slowing down to engage in wise speech and compassionate listening, such that we can let ourselves be known, tell each other what we need, and receive each other's truths in ways that heal hurts and build trust. You can find a few of guidelines for speaking and listening as radical friendship practices in chapters five and six of this book.

Wise action means engaging in ethical behavior and not causing harm. Traditionally, this means following five guidelines called the Five Precepts, which are framed as both actions to let go of and actions to take instead. They are:

1. Not killing, and instead—respecting life
2. Not stealing, and instead—taking only what is offered
3. Not lying, and instead—speaking truthfully, speaking from the heart
4. Not engaging in sexual misconduct, and instead—holding our own and each other's sexuality as sacred
5. Not getting intoxicated, and instead—prioritizing clarity

The precepts can be internalized in ever more subtle ways as we progress in our practice. If we truly live by them, we become the kind of people that others can trust. And perhaps even more importantly, we become the kind of people who can trust ourselves, with the confidence that when we extend ourselves in friendship, we become a clean, safe place for those we love.

Wise livelihood is the practice of earning our living and using our resources in a way that aligns with our ethical commitments. In the narrowest sense, wise livelihood refers to how we make our living. Early Buddhist texts warn practitioners against taking jobs that involve selling animals for slaughter, dealing weapons, trafficking humans, or dealing in alcohol or drugs. Basically, we want to avoid making our money through harming other beings or en-

abling others to do so. But because our globalized econo-
mies are so much more complex than during the Buddha's
time, the practice of wise livelihood today requires a more
rigorous examination of our role in harm or the alleviation
of harm, as well as how wealth and poverty are made and
maintained. Often this means looking upstream from our
work to explore where the money and resources you use
to do your work come from, as well as downstream—where
does the work you do go? Who does it ultimately benefit,
and who does it leave out? When we broaden our awareness
in this way, we expand the range of our radical friendship
to include people we may not know personally, but also
those who we love and believe in and want to thrive just
because we're all human beings and that means something.

The practice of wise livelihood also acknowledges that
we don't always have a whole lot of options for work that
doesn't involve harm of some kind. For example, when I
started to become more serious about my practice, I was
working nights as a cocktail waitress while going to college
during the day. When I learned about the ethical prohibi-
tion around selling alcohol, I began to feel bad about my
work. Making friends with myself in that moment meant
dropping self-judgment and seeing if it was possible for
me to do my work as ethically as possible. I did my best
to be kind to my co-workers and customers, even as I held
the aspiration to find work that was more in integrity with
my values (which I eventually did). When our options are
limited and we can't find work that causes no harm, wise
livelihood means doing the least harm possible.

MEDITATION The last wing of the Eightfold Path to liberation is about how we work with our minds. Our wise understanding and ethical behavior make settling our minds that much easier. It's pretty hard to meditate in the midst of delusion, and if we're in the habit of acting unskillfully, our minds will be constantly busy with worry and regret. Likewise, the meditative components of the Eightfold Path help us cultivate the inner resources that make the other path factors possible. This final pillar of the path is comprised of three elements: wise effort, wise mindfulness, and wise concentration.

Wise effort means applying the right quality and amount of energy that is needed for the task at hand. We often tend to interpret this as doing more, trying harder, and going all out in our friendships. But, it can also mean being sensitive to the moments when the right thing is actually to do less. When the Buddha taught this principle to a musician, he used the metaphor of tuning a stringed instrument. If the string is too loose, it makes a dull sound or no sound at all when played. If the string is too tight, it sounds shrill or breaks. So, the idea with wise energy is to be neither too tight nor too loose. With the right balance of tension and relaxation, we move through the world like beautiful music.

The reason to seek this kind of balance is because we want to cultivate the kind of effort that is sustainable. All too often, we can fall into cycles of pushing hard till we collapse, exhausted, only to get up once we catch our breath and do the same thing over again. This can show up in work in the form of burnout culture. It can show up in our politics, where we push hard for a big win and then crumble when we don't get the outcome that we hoped for. And it can show up in our friendships—doing the most to quickly get what we want in a relationship, and then getting discouraged when we don't immediately see the results of our actions. Wise effort has patience, and a healthy respect for the mystery of how things unfold. It too ebbs and flows, but on the whole, it is an effort that we can sustain over the long haul.

Wise mindfulness describes the capacity to direct our awareness in an intentional way. Our attention is valuable. Big businesses and political campaigns have huge budgets dedicated to capturing it. Formally practicing mindfulness through meditation restores our ability to choose to where we place our attention, and for what purpose. When we do this, we free our attention and restore our ability to focus on what really matters to us. adrienne maree brown, an author and facilitator of social movements, has referred to the practice of meditation as "attention liberation" on her blog. She writes:

> my life feels so different when i liberate my attention that it almost feels like the universe is gifting me attention reparations. instead of being frozen by hopelessness and fear for my species, which is often my reaction to the news, i experience a lot of days where i'm full of awe, laughter, and work that induces pride, noticing the small and massive miracles that are part of each day.[26]

There's freedom in being unfazed by the paper tiger, un-swayed by the shiny object, and able to connect with what we love in ourselves and each other. It's a choicefulness and agency we are all born with. And when we practice meditation, it grows.

Wise concentration is a faculty that allows us to sustain our awareness over time. If mindfulness is the ability to choose where we place our attention, then concentration is the power that gathers in the place where we keep it. It's not the concentration of pencil-biting and brow-furrowing, the kind you might have applied to a math problem on a standardized test. Rather, it's the *state of being* in which our mind, heart, and body are synchronized all in one place and at one time, so that there's a felt sense of being gathered, collected, unified, and whole. It's the experience of well-being that comes with learning to stay. And, in the practice of radical friendship, it's related to loyalty, faithfulness, and not abandoning ourselves and each other.

In both meditation and friendships, there can be so much power and intensity generated when we stay over time, it can be borderline uncomfortable. We find little ways to disperse our energy to make it less intense, like fid-geting or flaking out. There's nothing wrong with choosing to shift, as long as it's really a choice. *And,* there's something quite beautiful in staying with someone or something, al-lowing the power of our attention to become concentrated, and letting our friendship expand our capacity to be with the fullness that friendship contains.

PRACTICE
Wise Reflection

The Buddhist teacher Gina Sharpe describes the Eightfold Path as a holograph, pointing out that we can sometimes enter one of the steps and find ourselves smack in the middle of another one. The nonlinear nature of the path means that we rarely begin in the beginning, and that we never completely graduate. We just continue to include more of ourselves and more of our lives to be clarified within this simple framework such that eventually, there is no part of our lives that is not also a field for spiritual growth.

Doing what is hard to do, as the *Mitta Sutta* encourages us in this second quality of spiritual friendship, is infinitely harder when we don't know what work our friendships want and need from us. But, there is a way of reflecting on our lives that can teach us where to focus our attention, and what qualities we need to cultivate next. In Pali, the phrase is *yoniso manasikara*. It means something like "wise reflection," and etymologically, the *yoni-* prefix refers to the womb. The Buddhist teacher Thanissara translates *yoniso manasikara* as "in the womb of awareness," which, for me, sparks images of a warm, dark, and protected place where we can rest, dream, attend to the resonance of our experiences, and allow our innate wisdom to arise.

In a text called the *Yoniso Manasikara Sampada Sutta*, this activity of wise reflection is said to give rise to the

Eightfold Path of liberation in the same way that the dawn gives rise to the day.[27] Our reflection is at its wisest when it reflects the right balance of attention. Focusing only on suffering is a surefire ticket to Depression Town, where we can start to feel that humanity is so deeply flawed that we can never change. Focusing only on liberation certainly *feels* a lot better, but it can also keep us out of touch with our actual experience, leaving us a little deluded and probably more than a little annoying.

So, our practice is really to find the right balance of attention for *us*, which may not be exactly 50/50, given that we each come to the practice with a preexisting tendency to focus our attention one way or the other. In time, wise reflection on both our suffering and our liberation will lead to the confidence that there is nothing in our heart or experience that we need to fear or turn away from. We can make friends with all of it. We can cease to be at war with ourselves, and we can mine any experience we have in friendship, pleasant or unpleasant, for the wisdom that allows us to grow and change.

PRACTICE

Four Noble Truths Reflection

This reflection is intended as a systematic way to reflect on an experience of dukkha, or suffering, in a relational encounter, in a way that leads to wisdom and actionable next steps. I recommend you do this as a journaling practice, but it could also be a guided contemplation or a mindful speaking/listening exercise in pairs.

Challenge yourself to do this exercise at least twice: once for a scenario where you held the majority of the power or privilege relative to the person or people you were in relationship with, and again for a scenario where you were occupying a space that is oppressed by society. You can also return to it any time you are experiencing relational suffering and want to gain some insight into how it came to be, and how you can learn from it to have different experiences in the future.

First Noble Truth: Suffering (Dukkha)

Remember a time when you experienced suffering—as in stress, unsatisfactoriness, unreliability, or funkiness of any kind—in one or more of your friendships. What was the nature of the dukkha that arose? What did it feel like in your body, mind, and heart? Without trying to fix it for the moment, can you bring compassion to this experience right now?

Second Noble Truth: Clinging (Thanha)

Where is the clinging that led to this suffering? Are you holding any personal views, beliefs, or opinions that contributed to your experience? What about relational habit patterns showing up? Is it possible for you to identify the clinging and be responsible for your part without self-judgment or shame? Can you identify any systemic roots of this suffering? What role might racism, colorism, classism, homophobia, transphobia, ableism, misogyny, etc., be playing in your friendship?

Third Noble Truth: Freedom (Nibbana)

What would freedom from this particular kind of dukkha be like? How would it feel? Can you imagine a world in which you are free from the baggage of your personal and relational conditioning, free of clinging, fear, and shame? Can you imagine a world free from systems of oppression? How would living in such a world influence your relationship with other people? With yourself? Until we can create a world free of systemic oppression, is there a way you can imagine yourself being free even inside of these systems? What might that look and feel like?

Fourth Noble Truth: The Path (Magga)

What strategies or paths of practice have you engaged in to help you embody and move toward your vision of freedom? What's next in your freedom journey? You may want to include both internal/contemplative strategies as well as more external, action-oriented paths.

(4)

Endure What Is Hard to Endure

> Monks, a friend endowed with [this]
> quality is worth associating with . . .
> They endure what is hard to endure.
>
> —*Mitta Sutta*

ENDURANCE IS THE QUALITY of heart and mind that allows us not only to show up in loving relationship but also to *stay* in loving relationship. Even in harsh conditions. Even over long stretches of time. Authentic relationships take time to grow, and making friends is much more of a long-term practice than a one-time event.

According to the Buddhist teachings, we most often seek stability by solidifying our sense of self, what is sometimes called the "ego-mind." We try to source stability and endurance by finding a solid and unchanging sense of "me" in our physical characteristics, in the experiences we've lived, in the jobs we've worked, in the titles we've held, and in the things we love and hate and believe. There *is* a way of relating to these details of our lives that can support our endurance over time as radical friends. And, there's a way of relating to this being we call "me" that can make us temporarily *feel* more secure, but makes us more fragile in the long run.

When it comes to our sense of self (the self that we feel we are deep inside, the self that we present to the world), transforming fragility into stability is a spiritual practice of radical friendship.

This chapter is a meditation on true endurance. The kind that allows us to be both stable and flexible, to be confident in the simultaneous truths that we are amazing and beautiful just the way we are *and* that we still have room to grow. And, it's an exploration of three ways we can find an endurance that will truly support us on the radical friendship path: in our intentions, in our communities, and in our relationships with our ancestors and lineages.

CENTERING OUR HIGHEST INTENTIONS

One translation of the *Mitta Sutta* says that the spiritual friend is one who "endures harsh and ill-spoken words." I can assume that the Buddha would admit someone with the nickname "Yoga Bitch" into this category.

Yoga Bitch is what a particular clique of eleventh-grade girls repeatedly called me, under their breath, during my first year of teaching yoga and meditation in public high schools in New York City. I was thirty years old, but I felt a lot younger, fresh out of graduate school for an advanced degree I no longer intended to use. When I realized I wasn't cut out to be a career academic, a yoga studio near campus became my refuge from regret. Inside its pale pink walls with sitar music softly playing, no one asked me what my five-year plan was. We were in the present moment, this breath was all that mattered, and while my classmates focused on applying to PhD programs, I was becoming a Yoga Person. My identity as a failed graduate student receded, and a smug spiritual superiority floated up in its place.

When one of the studio owners asked me if I'd like an introduction to an organization that offered yoga classes in public schools, it felt like a sign from the cosmos. A surge of hope swelled in me. I longed for a job that would make me feel worthy of my own respect. If I could look good and noble to other people, perhaps I could actually feel that way on the inside.

My prior experience teaching yoga to kids had been years before, in a middle school after-school program. Those kids were young enough that they still wanted my approval, and because the after-school program had been optional, only the students who were really interested in yoga showed up. *How different could teaching in a high school be?* I thought. A lot different, as it turned out. Teenagers. Gym class. Mandatory. Oh, my . . .

On the first day of class, I played gentle electronic music in the background. One group of students asked me if it was a porn soundtrack. I began guiding a second round of Sun Salutations and the class protested, reminding me that they'd already *done* Downward-Facing Dog. I sputtered something about the power of repetition, but they had already flopped on the floor, motionless. In another class,

I demonstrated a backbend, and they screamed that I had camel toe (I did *not* have camel toe.) When we finally arrived at the end of class for our final relaxation meditation, my students chatted with their friends and played with their phones. All of them, alternating. So, when I went to quiet one group or ask them to put their phones away, the other group across the room would start again.

Thus began my year-long game of whack-a-mole—unruly teenager edition. But, because my self-love and sense of endurance were riding on my identity as a Good Yoga Teacher, I frantically tried to get my students to behave. I got snarky, attempting to control their behavior in an effort to control my self-image. I made more rules. I took it personally when no one followed them. And, when that group of eleventh-grade girls finally called me on it, their nickname for me—Yoga Bitch—really hit home. I cried. In front of the class. I never did earn their respect after that—I just did my best to preserve my dignity until the school year was over.

That school year gave me plenty of reasons to pause and reflect over the summer. In retrospect, I could see that my intentions had been a little mixed-up. It's not unusual, really, from the Buddhist perspective. When we do anything "good," we are almost always driven by a combination of wholesome motivations and self-seeking ones, and so it had been for me. I *did* genuinely want to share the yoga and meditation practices that had saved my heart and my sanity. They were skills I desperately wished I'd had as a teenager, skills that might have saved me a whole lot of anxiety and heartache growing up. But there was also this big part of me that craved my students' approval and wanted them to like me. As a teacher, you *cannot* need your students to make you feel good about yourself. It's just not their job.

Which brings me to another, related confusion. Because I was outnumbered—one of me, thirty of them—I felt like the victim of the students' behavior. Hence, the tears. But I was also the adult in the room, and as such, I held the power and would always ultimately have the upper hand. Sure, those eleventh-grade girls could hurt my feelings pretty badly, but I had the positional authority to get them suspended, botch their relationships with their parents, and bring down their GPAs. The school administration, security officers, and law enforcement would always be on my side. My students were never unaware of those facts, but I was. When I put myself in their shoes, their acting out felt like a totally understandable response to being in a restrictive and punitive school system all day long, and suddenly discovering a needy, weak link where they could act out their frustrations.

When our intentions are mixed, the Buddha's teachings invite us to use our mindfulness practice to center the highest, most wholesome one. In following our best intentions, in centering and re-centering them, the less-than-best ones get purified and begin to fall away.

While my intentions to be liked and seem spiritually evolved had unconsciously become my driving force, in my heart, I knew that these were not my *highest* intentions. My highest intentions were to create a place where high schoolers could enjoy a little space, take a few deep breaths, and get a good stretch on. I wanted to support their sustainability in a chaotic school environment. I wanted to create the container for a good experience with meditation and yoga so that if some day in the future they needed a deep breath and a good stretch, they would know how to get one. My highest intention was to be of maximum service.

It occurred to me that:

1. This could all be accomplished without requiring a single Downward-Facing Dog.
2. This could only be accomplished if I actually *modeled* the spaciousness, breath, and flexibility that I had been trying so heavy-handedly to demand from my students.

Everything changed once I stopped worrying about whether the students liked and respected me and I focused instead on how to embody the content I was trying to teach. Was it cool for them to call me Yoga Bitch? No, it was not. But it was *feedback*, and once I could hear it that way, it became less important to defend myself and more important to take in the information and use it to become a better teacher.

In my second year at the school, my classes held very little resemblance to what one would typically recognize as "yoga" or "meditation." I let my students chat, and I occasionally let them nap when they were super tired. In turn, they obliged me with a yoga pose or two and maintained relative quiet for guided meditation at the end of class. A few students got really into yoga practice, and I worked with them in small groups on more advanced poses. I gave those students mini-meditations to try at home and eventually trained them to be student teachers in the class. The majority of the teens never really took to yoga, but I felt pretty certain they knew I was an adult they could trust not to fly off the handle for small infractions or to make an example of them to prove a point. When my whole sense of worth wasn't hinging on whether other people (my students, my former classmates, my Facebook friends, my potential dates) thought I was spiritual, I had the space to be messy and to let my classroom be messy until I found a way of befriending my students that worked better for all of us.

Stepping into the unknown territory of building relationships across differences can make us feel vulnerable, even if we're the ones with the power. To feel more secure, more durable in who we are, we sometimes solidify around one particular aspect of our identity that we feel will be accepted and valued. The problem comes when circumstances challenge who we think we are, and we are so defensive of our sense of self that we are unable to incorporate new information about how we are showing up. Even good teachers have bad days, and even good allies make mistakes. If we've constructed our self-worth around always doing and saying exactly the thing that will gain approval from others, we'll be in major trouble when we inevitably create an impact that doesn't align with our intentions. We become defensive, or we collapse under the stress of being seen as different than we'd like to be.

Fragility is the opposite of endurance, and it's defined by the tendency to collapse when someone challenges who we think we are. The phrase "white fragility" was popularized by the sociologist Robin DiAngelo, who defines it as the inability of white people to tolerate racial stress. When confronted with the realities of racism, white people usually manifest fragility in the form of outrage at the suggestion that they benefit from privilege, or in demonstrations of woundedness that make it impossible to address the harms they have caused. This pattern of outrage or wounded denial is prominent in displays of whiteness, but it can also emerge with other forms of privilege. We can experience fragility around being straight, being male, being thin, being cisgender, or around any other identity that is automatically rewarded by society. Fragility rears its tender head when we become so defensive about the privilege we hold that we are unable to show up in radical friendship and mediate that privilege with wise action.

Where fragility coincides with institutionalized power, *that* is the place where we must build our endurance if we wish to show up as radical friends. Because the question isn't *whether* systems of oppression are playing out in our relationships. It's *how* are systems of oppression playing out in our relationships. No matter who we are, if we have spent time in a culture where there is ageism, racism, patriarchy, homophobia, transphobia, and ableism, we are navigating these societal -isms and -obias in our relationships in some way, consciously or not.

To be reliable, trustworthy friends (mentors, counselors, teachers, neighbors, employers), we need to grow our capacity to be with the discomfort of owning up to our power and of occasionally realizing we've been wielding it in ways we didn't mean to. Our confidence in that capacity to be with unpleasant realities and our clarity about our intentions to shift them are the best antidotes to fragility I know.

In Buddhist meditation, we expand our tolerance by noticing discomfort as simply that—discomfort. When we occupy a position of privilege—whether because of our rank, role, age, or other factors—we often hold the power to outsource our discomfort onto someone with less power. In meditation, we train in being present with our discomfort, connecting with the actual felt experience of the moment in all its intensity without deflecting or spilling our feelings out so that others have to clean them up. We train in simply feeling without falling into reactive patterns such as defending, blaming, or fixing. Mindfulness can give us the space to register the physical sensations—the ache in the chest, the tension in the jaw, the urge to run—and to know that what's happening is not actually a threat to anything we need to hold on to. What is threatened is a false sense of self, and when we can lighten up, even laugh at it, we become even more real in our radical friendships.

FINDING SANCTUARY IN COMMUNITY

In my work with organizations and communities, I often lead conversations to foster wider engagement and spark strategic change around diversity, equity, inclusion, and accessibility. At some point in the process, we usually divide into caucuses; we invite folks to separate into groups divided along the lines of whatever topic we're examining. If it's race, we'll likely divide up into a white group and a people of color group (sometimes dividing again for race or ethnicity). If it's gender, we'll separate into groups of women, men, and nonbinary people, or transgender and cisgender folks. It's a fairly common practice in this kind of work, and the intention is to make sure people who are marginalized by society have a space within the training where they *know* they will be centered. It's also for people in dominant groups to have a space to ask questions they fear are dumb, to express their thoughts and feelings with less of a filter, and not have to worry that their process will dominate the group space.

When we break into affinity groups, the dominant group *hates* it, and the marginalized group *loves* it—almost always.

Buddhist teacher Zenju Earthlyn Manuel, coined the phrase "cultural sanctuary" to describe these caucuses or affinity groups—spaces within spaces where people who share a marginalized identity gather together. We love them because, as Manuel puts it:

> The sanctuaries help us to voice and heal the suffering we have endured because of the misin-

terpretations and misconceptions based on our embodiments . . . To enter a sanctuary of healing is a way of tenderness—a way to provide needed compassion, perhaps a tender response to those treading an unfamiliar path.[28]

Sanctuary: a place of refuge or safety. The cultural sanctuaries that I belong to have been essential spaces of communion and ease, where I can access learning, process harm, and relax. They are spaces where those of us who share common experiences of oppression can practice freedom together, even in otherwise unfree places. Of course, these spaces aren't perfect. Sometimes there's disharmony due to drama or shade, and sometimes we're confronted with the tender truth that not one identity marker, not even the longest hyphenated combination, can ever really encompass all of who we are. And yet, when dukkha strikes within a cultural sanctuary, we don't have the pressure of trying to address it under and through the harmful paradigms of the dominant culture. When we're not spending energy answering, reckoning with, and performing for the mainstream, we have the freedom to actually focus on ourselves and each other. Having access to such a sanctuary bolsters our spirits so that we can endure the sometimes-harsh conditions we encounter outside of it.

For those of us who don't belong within a particular cultural sanctuary, the very existence of these groups can bring up feelings of being left out. We may not identify with the dominant culture group we technically belong to;

we may look at the other folks gathered in our caucus and think "These are not my people." It's beyond common for those of us holding privilege to be uncomfortable when that privilege is made visible by grouping us all together. Especially when we are doing our best not to cause harm, we may resent being lumped in with privileged folks who are just beginning their journey of waking up, who don't know or don't care about the power they wield in the world.

In these moments, we can regard the existence of cultural sanctuary as calling us into a different kind of belonging—supporting the sanctuary of our friends by honoring their sacred spaces. When those of us in the dominant culture are willing to move into the discomfort of feeling left out or having our privilege made visible, we make space for marginalized people to move into a greater degree of safety and communion. Seeing the happiness and ease that these sanctuaries create makes it easier to protect these spaces wholeheartedly. We all need spaces that we belong inside and we can be centered within. Taking pleasure in defending those spaces for people who never get to have that experience within dominant culture is a way of belonging too. Radical friendship means believing people who have been marginalized by society when they tell us what they need and doing our best to ensure that those needs are met.

For the Buddha, the capacity for rejoicing in someone else's joy is among the highest forms of love. In the texts, it's referred to as *mudita*, or sympathetic joy, and it's one of the boundless, divine qualities of heart and mind that are natural manifestations of the awakening heart. Mudita is one of the hardest kinds of love to practice because when we see someone else's joy, our own feelings of scarcity and lack can get triggered. It takes real mental discipline not to slide from witnessing the happiness of other people into asking, *But what about me?*

Mudita, the contentment we feel in witnessing someone else's joy, is an abundant kind of love, a love imbued with the wisdom that we all belong, and we can all belong differently. On the path of radical friendship, this heart quality is our best resource when we feel hurt or left out of an oppressed group's sanctuary space. It helps us to endure those feelings, which can be hard to bear, by finding our comfort in the sense of collective well-being. It is a way of loving ourselves that expands our sense of self that is beyond our individual experience and into our innate interrelatedness. We feel we have enough, we feel we are enough, and that enoughness powers an endurance that keeps us in community.

THE ENDURANCE OF OUR ANCESTORS

One of the biggest differences between Western-convert Buddhism and heritage-Buddhist communities is that in the mainstream Western adaptation, there's a marked absence of rituals to honor and connect with our ancestors. In the Buddha's time, the presence of ancestors and the recognition of their role in society was a part of the cultural fabric of everyday life. But for the white Western students who traveled to Asia in the 1960s and 1970s to learn Buddhism, their own ancestries, family lineages, and cultural traditions were things they were trying to get *away* from. They didn't feel like sources of power—they felt like sites of repression and shame. When they returned to the West and began teaching what they felt was the essence of Buddhist practices, many aspects of ritual culture—including those that honor ancestors—were left out of their transmission of the teachings.

For those of us whose ancestors were most deeply affected by the violence and domination of empire, lineage isn't something we're trying to get away from. It's something we're trying to get back to. Colonization taught us to fear witchcraft, ghosts, and juju. We were told that the spirit world wasn't real, that relating to it was a sign of unenlightened superstition. We were warned that the unseen realms were full of evil, that to invite connection with beings who have passed on is to open the door to disaster. Fraying our connections to our ancestral homes and practices made it easier for the agents of empire to seize our land, our labor, and our bodies.

Fortunately, our ancestors have not gone. At the very least, they are present in every cell in our bodies, coded into our DNA. The air we breathe contains particles that at one time hovered in their lungs. The blood in our veins flows with droplets of water that once ran through theirs. We may have pictures, stories, or objects they once owned to remember them by. If we're lucky, we may be able to connect with them through an insight, an intuition, or a gut feeling. In the decolonial view, our ancestors are not out to get us. Many of them want to help us, and some of them need our help too. They want to be in relationship with us, and to make friends with them is to make friends with a vital resource that extends beyond the material realm. To restore right relationships on this planet, our ancestors are a source of wisdom and power that we desperately need.

When I wanted to deepen my relationship with the ancestors as a part of my spiritual practice, I sought out a priest in an African diasporic tradition called Lucumí (which, incidentally, means "friend" in the Yoruba-based liturgical language of that tradition). The priest suggested I create an ancestor altar on a low table covered in white cloth and that I place a potted plant on the altar to represent life. He gave me the assignment of talking to the elders in my family and finding out whatever they could remember about our ancestors—their names, the places they lived, what kinds of food they liked, what they did for a living, what they did for fun, etc. He also told me to gather whatever kinds of artifacts I could and place them on the altar, whether they were photos or objects my ancestors actually owned, or modern objects like pens, paper, cigars, flowers, knitting needles, or other things they would have enjoyed.

When I'd gathered my objects, I had a moment of hesitation that I tried to explain to him. "I . . . don't think my ancestors want to be on the altar, you know, *all together.*" I gestured from one side of the table to the other, my hand crossing the invisible line that divided the Black and white faces. The priest spoke patiently with me. "They already are," he said. "Their altar is you."

Many of us have ancestors who we're not so proud of. Some of them did things *they* weren't proud either of in the name of survival. Some of them were so deluded they couldn't see that what they were doing was wrong. Some of them had been so deeply wounded that they hurt others in turn. The way we each live our lives now, in this lifetime, has the power to make right the wrongs of the past. We can think of this as healing our ancestors who caused harm and making amends by vowing to live differently than they did.

When we call on our ancestors for help and support though, we must call on the ones who were courageous, compassionate, bold, and free in their hearts. We must call on the ones who loved us, dreamed of us, and fought for us before we were born, who did their best to create a world they'd be proud for us to inherit. The ones who the Buddhist teacher Ruth King calls our "wise and bright ancestors." We all have ancestors like these, every one of us, and it doesn't matter one bit whether we know their names. Whether they are ancestors of our family or ancestors of our spirit lineages, we can call on them for support and protection in difficult times, asking them to be by our sides, to keep watch at our backs, and to whisper in our ears. We can live in a way that continues to make them proud. And we can rest for them, heal for them, and take a deep breath for them now, as so many of them never got a chance to do when they were alive.

It gives me great hope to think that our ancestors can still, through the altars of our lives, embody new ways of being together in whatever realm they exist in now. May their guidance help us to endure these turbulent times and find new ways of being together here on Earth.

PRACTICE

Endurance through Praise and Blame

Note: You can take this contemplation as a meditation or journaling exercise. Either way, begin and end with a few minutes of gathering and settling the mind.

Remember a time when you were praised for your efforts in showing up for someone else's well-being or freedom—an individual or a community. Picture in your mind's eye where you were, what it looked/felt like, who else was there. Remember what was said or done that signaled you were being praised or admired for your actions. What does it feel like in your body as you mentally reconstruct this scene? How about your mind? If you find a sense of warmth, relaxation, ease, or joy, recognize that, take it in, and mentally note, *This is pleasant. Mm! Pleasant.* Notice, too, any desire to get more of that feeling or any sense of self that arises in response to the pleasure of the memory. See if you can soften the urge to pull for more of that feeling and just enjoy it with a sense of openness. *Being praised, being liked, being seen for my good intentions and actions = pleasant.* Imagine that this moment and the pleasant energy that comes with it is like a great, wispy cloud passing through the big blue sky of your mind.

Now, remember a time when you suddenly realized that you weren't showing up as the radical friend you had intended to be—either through your own insight or by being called out by someone else. Using your imagination, recall that moment as clearly as you can: where you were, what it looked and felt like, who else was there, how they responded to you, and how you responded to them. Notice how it feels in your body to return to this scene and what thoughts or story lines begin to play through your mind. Be aware of any tension, sensations of sinking or shrinking, or urges to push away. Mentally note, *Wow, this is truly unpleasant. I do not like this feeling.* Observe the tendency of the mind to defend, attack, or blame to deflect the unpleasant experience. Notice if there's a sense of self, a "me" that is born in that reflection—one who is bad or wrong or who has been wronged by others. See if it's possible to let go of the identification with the feeling, or the story, or the desire to push it away, and attend to the unpleasantness itself with compassionate awareness. *Unpleasant is like this.* Like another cloud passing through the big blue sky of your mind.

Do this a few times, alternating between the pleasant and unpleasant experiences, getting to know your own mental, emotional, and physiological responses to being praised as a great friend or blamed as a crappy one. What wisdom can you distill from this experience?

Finally, let your awareness expand to encompass both experiences at once—the sense of having shown up in friendships in ways that you are really proud of and also in ways that are slightly cringe-worthy. As you hold both experiences in your attention, know that this is just what the journey of radical friendship is like: not always pleasant in the conventional sense, but expansive and deeply rewarding nonetheless. As you rest in this knowing, see if you can articulate an intention for yourself that will help you find endurance within the ups and downs of this path of practice. When you bring this contemplation to a close, write down the word or phrase that came up for you regarding your own highest intention on the path of radical friendship. Keep it somewhere close so you can return to it for motivation, to help you keep going even through the sometimes less-than-pleasant awakenings along the way.

PRACTICE

Mudita (Sympathetic Joy)

Mudita can be practiced on the spot to remedy moments of feeling scarcity and lack, and it can also be practiced as a formal contemplation to grow our capacity for experiencing joy in each other's joy.

To cultivate mudita for groups, start by thinking of a group you don't personally belong to, one that seeks sanctuary space as respite from the ignorance or hostility of the dominant culture.

Imagine this group of people in a beautiful, warm, protected space where the members have everything they need to feel safe and joyful in shared community.

As you imagine them—happy, free, and at ease on their own terms—send them this phrase right from your heart to theirs:

May your joy continue to grow and bless your lives.

Repeat this phrase several times in a spacious way. Imagine the group receiving your wish as a light that adds another layer of warmth, protection, and care to the space. Imagine their joy increasing as a result of your anonymous wish. Feel how good it can be to send your love and support without needing anything in return. Center that feeling with your awareness; let its imprint register in your system. Know that you can return to this practice and this feeling anytime you wish as an alternative option to feeling jealous or left out.

(5)

Tell Secrets

Monks, a friend endowed with [this]
quality is worth associating with. . . .
They tell you their secrets.

—*Mitta Sutta*

SECRETS ARE THE TRUTHS of our inner lives, and speech is
the bridge that brings these truths out and into the open. In
the practice of radical friendship, "telling our secrets" is how
we allow ourselves to be seen and known. In this line of the
Mitta Sutta, I hear the Buddha encouraging each of us to give
voice to our unique way of experiencing and understanding
the world so that the people who love us can witness us and,
when need be, support us, join us, or have our backs.

Telling secrets is not just about getting something off
our chests. It's also about exposing societal truths that
need to change. When the secrets we keep conceal our
honest, lived experiences, then remaining silent holds us
back from the liberated friendships we seek. If we never
let on when we've been harmed, then those harms have
no chance of being amended. If we never admit when

we've made a mistake, then our friends can't rely on us to be accountable and learn from our experiences. And, if we never reveal what we believe, what we care about, and who we truly are, then we deprive the world of our unique loveliness and we deprive ourselves of seeing that loveliness reflected back to us in the eyes of our friends.

That said, it's not hard to understand why some of us might hesitate to tell our secrets and speak our truths. Historically, it has been strictly taboo to share, even among friends, our thoughts and experiences with money, politics, sex, health, and so many other intimate and real facts of every human life. While the culture is changing and we're generally becoming more open about subjects that used to be undiscussable, when we openly challenge existing power structures, our words are often dismissed as rude or inappropriate. Taboos and etiquette around speech—whether at home, at school, or at work—often serve to reinforce the status quo.

Then there's the fear of the "callout"—the possibility of being publicly outed and called to task when we've messed up in some way. All kinds of offenses can get you called out, ranging from mildly misguided political analysis all the way to serious instances of bodily and psychological harm. Behavior that was accepted in the past has become unacceptable, and today when we speak up, the world is so much more ready to listen. I believe that this is a good thing on the whole, but I also think it's sometimes murky territory on the spiritual path. What kind of offense or harm is callout-worthy? Who do we call out, who do we let slide, and why? What is the intention that guides us to publicly tell those truths, or to privately pull someone aside, or to let it go and say nothing at all? In terms of spiritual friendship, the inner place from where we source our speech matters just as much as what we say and who we say it to.

When there is a hard truth I need to share, in person or online, I turn to the guidelines on wise speech to help me do it. These four questions drawn from the Buddha's teachings have been a tremendous resource for me in developing an intuitive sense of which secrets or truths I choose to reveal, and when and how to do so. They also help me quiet my worries about how what I have to say might be received which, more often than not, would lead to me saying nothing at all.

CONTEMPLATIONS ON WISE SPEECH

1. Is it true?
2. Is it kind?
3. Is it unifying?
4. Is it meaningful?

Especially if we feel a bit of hesitation in our bodies or doubt in our minds as we are about to speak, these questions can help us clarify where that hesitation is coming from.

Is it our social conditioning to appease or conform?

Is it just not the right place, time, or person with whom to share?

Is there a fear of being rejected for who we are and how we experience the world?

If nothing else, these contemplations on wise speech slow us down, affording us the time to stay in our integrity—a gesture of spiritual friendship to ourselves as well as other people. And, if we've already spoken up and it didn't go so well, we can use these questions as a basis for reflection to learn from our experience and deepen our practice.

Is It True?

It wasn't until I was nineteen and halfway across the country that I found my first queer relationship. "Best friend," I lied over the phone to my mom one Sunday night, having spent the afternoon in my girlfriend's arms, dancing at a gay salsa club in the Mission District in San Francisco. "Roommate," I added a few years later, referring to another girlfriend, my first true love. We lived together for two years—packing lunches, wiping tears, giggling, spooning—and my parents had no idea.

It was difficult for me to just *say* it, so I tried to signal queerness in other ways. I cut my hair and took to wearing overalls and cargo pants. My queer friends lovingly joked that I looked like I was in drag. My fashion power-place has always been red lipstick and wispy fabrics, which has meant that in mainstream spaces I mostly pass for straight. Even in cargo pants. Unless, of course, I choose to come out.

The privilege of passing for straight is that, for me, coming out is *always* a choice, especially now that I'm partnered up with a straight, cisgender man. It's a choice, for example, to refer to "my ex-*girlfriend*" or simply "my ex" when telling a story to a fellow mom on the playground. I can reason with myself that bringing up the whole "I used to date women" thing is gratuitous in such a casual encounter. It's annoying, isn't it, when people insist on signaling their queerness ("This one time in college . . . ") even when they're living what appears to be a totally hetero life? But then later than night, I wonder why I still feel like nobody knows me, and why it's taking so long to make real friends in my new city.

Why do we omit key information, when it comes to sharing the truths of our lived experiences? Well, because the stakes can be high. Our experience of the world is so often shaped by the circumstances of our birth and life—rich or poor, documented or undocumented, formally educated or not, queer or straight—and many of us have secrets associated with these experiences. With every coming-out, we take the risk that the truth of who we are will cost us the relationships we want. Or worse, that our truths will somehow be weaponized against us.

As a radical friendship practice, telling our secrets isn't limited to coming out about our sexual orientation. For some of us, our political views, economic class, mental illnesses, addictions, or disabilities are mostly invisible to others unless we make them known. We might not want to go shouting them from the rooftops or blasting them across social media for a variety of good reasons—employability, safety, and so on. But, when we do feel safe enough to tell these secrets, to disclose our unseen identities, experiences, and beliefs, we make more space for ourselves in our relationships, more space for ourselves in the world. We get to see who will show up for us. We get to experience the satisfaction of being truly known. And, the people who love us receive the gift of truly knowing us too.

I did eventually come out to my mom, when I was about twenty-five. And last year, almost fifteen years later, I called her up to remind her on September 23. "Happy Bisexual Visibility Day!" I shouted when she picked up. "Just wanted to let you know I'm still at least half gay." She squealed and thanked me, then asked how my day was going. I told her about how important it felt to be celebrating this holiday, to locate my sexuality in how I experience the world, in how I continue to prioritize true love and intimacy with friends and chosen family, and not just in my relationship with my partner. She marveled at how different sexuality is now than back in her day when she thought she had only two options—straight and lesbian. "You're so lucky," she said. *I am lucky*, I thought.

When we claim our truths in radical friendship, we make more space for others to claim theirs too. If everyone who was even a little bit gay came out, there would be a lot more people who realize their favorite neighbor, beloved niece, or best professor ever is part of a group of people they otherwise claim to hate. The same is true for those of us who have other kinds of identities or experiences that are less visible—disabilities, gender expressions, education levels, class backgrounds, and so forth. When we're not out, the discomfort is on us alone, and frankly being marginalized within society is already uncomfortable enough. When we're out, our experience becomes a shared one. If there's enough love to mediate it, the discomfort of sharing can be not only productive but also transformative, for speaker and listener alike.

Perhaps, most importantly of all: for people like me, choosing to come out can help make the world safer for people who are just like us, but who don't have the luxury of passing.

When I'm about to reveal a truth that involves a coming-out of some kind, my temperature rises. My ears turn red, and sometimes my neck starts to flush. I can hear my own heartbeat quickening. My chest tightens, and my throat gets dry. It's in these moments that the contemplation *Is it true?* becomes super, super important. If I were to believe that physical comfort alone is a sign that I'm on the right track, I would probably keep my mouth shut. But, if I ask myself, *Is it true?* and the answer is a resounding yes, I know that the physical discomfort is a signal that I'm about to do something new. And probably, brave.

Is It Kind?

"I'm not attracted to you, and I don't want to be your friend."

This is, I'm afraid, the exact text message I once sent to a very nice person with whom I had no chemistry when they asked me for a second date.

In my defense, I was new to the whole boundaries game. I was trying to break a streak of ill-suited relationships that I'd landed in simply because I couldn't say no. I was

123

learning, slowly, that even if someone wanted to spend time with *me*, that did not mean I was obligated to spend time with *them*. My new therapist was walking me through this revelation and encouraging me to bring voice to these new perspectives. To stop evading calls and inventing other plans and to find my True No.

Apparently, I found it.

And then some.

The Buddha encourages us that when we tell our truths to do so with kindness. But, when we're new at telling the whole truth, we're often a little heavy-handed the first few times. It was an important step in my friendship with myself to share my true feelings with this person who wanted a second date rather than being evasive and avoidant and keeping these feelings secret. Years later, I had the opportunity to apologize for being so blunt. If I could do it again, I would definitely offer the same message—with a softer delivery. When I finally did apologize, I did so knowing that while what I said was messy and rude, it was also the kindest thing I could manage at the time: to tell the truth a little clumsily instead of stringing yet another person along, and abandoning myself in the process.

The question "Is it kind?" invites us into a more expansive definition of kindness in our friendships and all of our relationships. Being kind is not the same as being nice. Kindness is saying or doing what causes the least possible amount of harm over the long term. Which means that, between friends, it is possible to exchange words that are both extremely kind and a little difficult to hear. The truth is disruptive by definition. But, the benefits of saying what needs to be said are so much greater than the momentary discomfort in bringing our truth to light.

It does seem to help the message land well if we can connect with our *intention* to be kind. We can even begin by stating our intention out loud: *I bring this up because I care about your well-being.* Or, *Because we have a shared commitment to justice* . . . Or, *Because I want us to continue to have an honest relationship* . . . Or, *Because I trust you* . . .

When we tell secrets that we fear may land hard with another person, we often brace our muscles, armoring the space in front of our hearts. To tell your truth with kindness, soften the front of your body, if you can. Our anticipatory defensiveness can signal to our listener that they should get defensive too. So, relax your jaw, relax your throat. Among friends, love is your best protection.

If we or someone we care about has been harmed, or if we have been conditioned to keep those truths secret, our phrasing or tone may be a little strong while we're finding our voice. But, this doesn't mean that if we can't say something nicely, we shouldn't say it at all. Kindness is not just speaking in soft, soothing tones. For those of us who have made a practice of silently metabolizing our suffering, radical friendship often means making some noise.

Is It Unifying?

The Buddha's teachings on wise speech ask us to refrain from divisive speech. It's a reminder that, as radical friends, we try to tell our truths in ways that do not intentionally pit people against one another, creating an us-versus-them culture within or between communities. And, this principle of wise speech comes into tension with what we think of as "callout culture"—the practice of publicly exposing someone who has caused harm (usually on social media or some other widely distributable electronic media format). Most often, it's exposing an interpersonal harm (or pattern of harm) that reveals a person who we *thought* was woke is actually an agent of structural violence of some kind. Most often, it does have the quality of telling a secret, airing something that has been only privately known into public space. The person who has committed harm is called out into the open, and we, who are now witnesses to that harm, are called to turn our backs on them.

Now, it must be said that one of the characteristics of supremacy culture is an aversion to open conflict. And, within this particular cultural frame, it's considered divisive to just *point out* ways how individuals or groups may be perpetuating systemic injustice through their behaviors, policies, and structures. If we come forward to share our experiences of how we've been negatively affected, or voice our concerns about how a person or community may affect others, there's always a risk that people in power will feel personally criticized or threatened. When that happens, the person sharing their experience is often made out to be *the cause* of that experience.

So, when it comes to telling secrets that involve our experiences of harm, speaking in a unifying way is not so simple as it might at first sound. Faced with the threat of be-

ing seen as divisive, being written off as the "angry _____
person" with a chip on their shoulder, we may choose to
silence ourselves rather than risk being ostracized by our
communities, or worse—not believed by them. I know this
has been the case with me.

Many years ago, I was one of a trio of Black women who
took the lead on organizing a "meditation occupation" of an
intersection in downtown Brooklyn. We met through a larger
network of leaders who were brainstorming how to activate
spiritual practice and action in service of social justice. When
a labor organizer approached the group with a request for
support in the Fair Wages movement, the three of us stepped
up to make it happen. In the months before the action, we
did a series of teach-ins at Buddhist centers, yoga studios, and
wellness spaces in New York, asking organizers and worker/
activists to join us and tell the story of their campaign for a
living wage, the Fight for $15. The three of us worked hard to
articulate the bridge between their struggle and our practice,
and to offer mindful communities who were committed to
generosity and compassion a chance to move boldly into wise
action. Our invitation was this: instead of meditating alone
at home, come join us for a meditation in the streets, and
use your practice to block traffic and raise awareness about
the campaign for a living wage.

On the chilly morning of the action, dozens of meditators arrived at our meeting place, the Brooklyn Zen Center,
for hot coffee and conversation—the vast majority of them
folks that myself and the two other lead organizers had
personally connected with and asked to come. Along with

them arrived one of the members of that larger network of leaders, a white woman, who had offered to document the event. Her staff handed out branded t-shirts with the name of her nascent organization emblazoned on the front. The camera crew she brought along interviewed her and her staff in the crowd of people—but they never asked to speak to me or the other two Black women who had put so much heart and energy into launching this event.

The meditation occupation was successful: we shut down traffic for several minutes and generated some compelling images of a diverse group of people sitting cross-legged, eyes closed, holding signs that read "Sit for $15." Later, I learned that the footage the camera crew had shot was being used to frame the action as the launch event for a new organization founded by the woman who showed up after all the groundwork had been done. The people who my partners and I had recruited to attend had been there to support fair wages, not to become colorful poster children for the launch of a glossy new wellness initiative. The whole thing seemed dishonest, and I felt we'd been used.

A few months later, her lead staff person approached me to "partner" with them on another project. I declined. I expressed my hurt and disappointment about the launch video they had produced, which claimed ownership of work they simply hadn't done. She apologized for the video, but explained that they had spent a lot of money producing it and they would not take it down. She also asked me to keep my feelings about her, and about her organization, to myself. After all, she reasoned, we're all working toward the same goal, right? No need to create divisions here. And anyway, she reminded me, *no one likes a shit talker.*

I told her I'd share my experience with whoever I wanted to. But I didn't. Instead, I quietly witnessed that staff person's rise to prominence in radical communities I cared deeply about. I looked on in confusion as she forged public partnerships with folks whose integrity I deeply respected. I said nothing when her name came up in conversation, I went out of my way to avoid her in social gatherings, and over time, I began to doubt my experience. Maybe what she did wasn't so bad? Maybe she had changed?

Eventually, she got called out for what turned out not to be a one-off incident, but a pattern of behavior. It happened years later, and not by me. A former employee, another Black woman, wrote a blog post documenting multiple instances of racist, able-ist, dominating behavior she experienced and witnessed while working for this person. As it turns out, there were many Black women out there with similar stories. As their stories rolled in to the comments section of that original blog post, it became apparent that there had actually been multiple, repeated private call-ins with this leader over the years, resulting in accountability circles, advisory boards, and other attempts to remediate and repair harm. None of this had changed her behavior in any meaningful way. Now, prominent Black women leaders were calling for her resignation from the new organization she had founded. In a matter of days, she issued a public apology and stepped down.

In her book *Talking Back: Thinking Feminist, Thinking Black*, the feminist scholar bell hooks wrote, "When we end our silence, when we speak in a liberated voice, our words connect us with anyone, anywhere who lives in silence." I'm so grateful to the writer of that callout piece, and to the people who stepped in to share their experiences alongside. We don't know each other, but I received their words as gestures of radical friendship. I started writing my own comment several times and couldn't bring myself to press "send." I imagine many others wanted to step forward and share their stories also, but didn't, for any number of reasons. The people who *did* speak up helped me to understand and feel that I wasn't alone. The shame, self-doubt, and confusion I'd held onto for years after she'd co-opted our work began to lift when they raised their voices.

Why was I so afraid of speaking up all that time? Well, for one thing, I didn't want to risk being seen by the wider community as petty or divisive. People who I totally respected seemed to want and be helped by the offerings she was putting into the world. Seeing this, I had a hard time assessing whether what happened to me was even worth mentioning. Was what happened just a fluke, an early misstep from which she had since grown and changed? Was I just a hater, jealous of her rising success? I didn't want to be one of those people who sits on the sidelines, waiting to tear generally good leaders to shreds for the mildest of infractions.

Which brings me to the source of my second hesitation: I didn't *really* want to hurt her just because she'd hurt me. I didn't want to harm her, but I also didn't want to be in a position to be harmed by her again, and I always did wonder if she was still exploiting women of color behind the scenes. Was it my responsibility to warn others? Was it better to let them find out for themselves? Deeper still was the fear that even if I did share my experience, I wouldn't be believed.

Thankfully, when it comes to telling secrets that have the potential to build unity and initiate needed change, we have more options than the "call-in" and the "callout." Radical friendship opens up a third space, where we can confide in a closer circle, with people we trust. We gain confidence and clarity when we speak with folks we know will be there for us regardless if they think we are overreacting, who won't judge us even if our motives are murky or mixed. Our friends can help us stay close to our desire to make things right and prevent future harm. And they can help us decide whether a call-in, a callout, or something else is needed to achieve our goals. I wish I'd talked to trusted friends about what happened sooner.

In the end, we can't control how others will receive what we have to say. People may think we're haters. We may not be believed. We may be blamed. But, we can always source our speech from a place that looks and longs for connection, even as we articulate the divisions that also exist. And we can stay close to the people who believe us, support us, and have our backs while we tell the truth that is ours to tell.

Is It Meaningful?

The last contemplation on wise speech asks us to refrain from what's classically called "idle speech," or gossip, which is the act of telling somebody else's secrets. Most of the time when we share truths that are not our own, we are trying to form a bond with someone while avoiding the risk of actually sharing about ourselves. When our habit is to discuss other people's missteps or misfortunes, it can be out of genuine concern or need, or it can be a subtle way of making ourselves superior to them. Gossip robs us of the true intimacy that is available in any encounter when we share from our own experience in the present moment.

Of course, idle speech isn't strictly limited to gossip. It can also be the result of feeling discomfort, or a lack of confidence. There may be an elephant in the room of a friendship we've cultivated for years, but rather than acknowledging it, we go on making small talk. We stick to topics that feel safe rather than treading into territory that, while it may be momentarily uncomfortable, could also be life-alteringly profound if we find the will to say what needs to be said.

One of my longest continuous friendships today is with someone who took the chance to tell me she thought I needed help. We'd been friends for about five years at that point, and while I'd long since started my spiritual journey, I was still partying like a rock star. Or, so I thought. Eventually, I learned that I was still partying like an out-of-control teenager, long after many of my oldest friends had cleaned up their acts. After an especially saucy evening, when this particular friend told me she thought I had a drinking problem, I laughed. I didn't have a problem, I told her. I was awesome. I was hilarious. I was the life of the party!

I never unheard those words, though. *I think you have a drinking problem.* . . . They gnawed at me, and the more I looked to my life for evidence that it wasn't true, the more I recognized it just might be. After an especially embarrassing incident where I'd had one (read: *several*) too many drinks, I decided it couldn't hurt to check out an alcoholism recovery program. There was a part of me that still just wanted to prove my friend wrong, but I knew taking a break from drinking for a while couldn't hurt. What I didn't know was how much better my life would become when I put down intoxicants for good.

Turns out, she was right.

What was truly wild was how my other friends responded when I shared that I'd quit drinking. "Oh, thank God," they gasped. I can't tell you how many people confessed that they too had been concerned, or that they had simply pulled back from our friendship because they were sick of taking care of me or cleaning up my messes when we went out. *Why didn't you tell me?* I moaned again and again. It felt like I'd had a piece of broccoli stuck in my teeth for the better part of a decade, and most of my friends just let me walk around grinning like an idiot.

In the end, I knew that my behavior was my own responsibility, and that it's not my friends' job to save me from my choices. But I do think that was the difference between the majority of my friendships and this truly radical bestie of mine: she wasn't willing to let me go out like that without letting me know what she saw, and she did it with love, in a place and time when I could really hear her. For that, I'm eternally grateful.

Engaging in meaningful speech doesn't mean every word we say has to be deep and profound. Especially when we're just beginning to make friends with someone, small talk can be hugely meaningful. We can start with hello, ask questions about how they like the weather, where they're from, what movies they've enjoyed lately, and so forth. When we're remarking on a common experience or joking around, the secret we're telling isn't so much in the content of our words. It's our wish to connect, and we can share that wish not only with our words but also with the shine in our eyes, in small gestures of kindness, and in our willingness to make the first move toward making a new friend.

Sometimes idle speech is a way of avoiding awkward silence. There's nothing wrong with saying a few words to put ourselves or others at ease, but there's also nothing wrong with a moment of quiet. Being a human being is awkward a lot of the time. We don't know what to say, what to do with our hands; half the time, we don't know what the hell is going on at all. No one ever died of awkwardness as far as I know, but the things we do to cover up the truth of our awkwardness can undermine our intentions to reveal who and how we really are.

Awkwardness is beautiful and genuine when we just accept it for what it is. If we can be there in the human experience of not knowing what comes next, and if we can relax and hang in there together, something always emerges eventually. Something we can't calculate, can't force. In moments like these, our practice is to resist the temptation to hide our uncertainty, to resist anxiously filling the space with words that mean less than the silence does. Because if we rush to fill that space with whatever we think belongs there, we might miss whatever the universe had in mind, which is often more precise, brilliant, and real than what we might have expected. The speech that comes through us after that awkward pause, the words that spill out of not knowing what to say—these are the vulnerable, sensitive words that can often share something completely fresh and of the moment. When we wait for what is truly meaningful to come through, we often end up speaking something that needs to be said and can *only* be said by us, right now. Those words mean the world—and they are worth waiting for.

PRACTICE

Wise Inner and Outer Speech

Training in wise speech begins with paying attention to our thoughts, which are a kind of inner speech. As we settle into meditation, some of our thought-streams will consist of whole conversations with another person, carried out entirely in our minds. Sometimes, these will be do-overs of conversations we've already had, where we mentally improve upon what actually happened so that everyone says just the right thing. We'll also have fantasies of future conversations, the ones we want to have, but haven't yet.

If a particular conversation comes up once or twice while we're meditating and it's fairly easy to drop it and come back to our chosen practice, we should let it go. But, if every time the mind wanders it defaults to rehearsing or rehashing something we'd like to say, it may be a moment of inner speech that needs a bit of attention. Some persistent patterns of internal dialogue need to be explored before they're ready to fade into the background.

When you suddenly notice that you're having that same old mental conversation yet again, whether it's during meditation or while going about your day, one option is to pause and mentally note what is happening right now: *inner speech*. As with any sensory phenomenon that arises during meditation, becoming aware of what's happening in the present moment counts as practice. When we're having conversations in our mind, we lose track of time, we lose sensation in our bodies, and sometimes we feel as if we're somewhere else. But even while we're lost in thought, we're creating patterns of inner speech that eventually often manifest outwardly. But, if we're aware of inner speech as it arises, we're less likely to be lost in the virtual reality of our own imagination, and less likely to create patterns of thought and speech that are outside of our intentions.

Before you go back to your meditation practice or whatever activity you were engaged in, take a few moments to investigate your inner dialogue:

- **Is it true?** Is what you imagine yourself saying factually true, or is it more like something you wish was true? Does the way you express yourself in your mind feel aligned with your true intentions?

- **Is it kind?** Are you using this fantasy as a way to say things you'd never say out loud? How does it feel in your body and mind to imagine speaking this way? Pleasant, unpleasant, neutral, some combination? What do you imagine the impact might be—on you, on others—if you said these things in real life?

- **Is it unifying?** Is this imaginary conversation one in which you forge a connection? Create a boundary? Emphasize sameness? Emphasize difference? What can you learn from your answers to these questions?

- **Is it meaningful?** Are you meeting some need by imagining yourself speaking this way? Is there a kind way to meet this need in real life?

After you've spent a few moments exploring the inner dialogue and mentally noting any insights that occur to you about the nature of it, see if you can return to full presence with your meditation or the task at hand. Take whatever insights arose into your next conversation.

(6)

Keep Secrets

Monks, a friend endowed with [this]
quality is worth associating with . . .
They keep your secrets.

—*Mitta Sutta*

IN THE LAST CHAPTER, we defined secrets as the intimate
truths of who we are—our histories, lived experiences, and
dreams for our relationships and the world we long to build
together.

Keeping secrets is the act of *receiving* these intimate truths
from one another, and how well we hold those truths when
we receive them. It's how we listen, and how we respond
when those secrets or truths are shared with us. Building
trust within friendships has everything to do with how we
receive each other as we reveal how we experience our relationships and the world we share. Wise speech is only half of
the equation when it comes to liberating communication—
and some would say, the less important half.

In his book *The Heart of the Buddha's Teaching*, the Viet-
namese Zen Buddhist monk Thich Nhat Hanh's chapter

on wise speech is almost entirely devoted to the practice of compassionate listening. He suggests that when we develop our capacity for deep listening, we are learning to relieve the other person of their suffering, and to listen to them into their own wisdom. When we listen with complete confidence that the person telling their story has everything they need to fully awaken, our listening becomes a force for their healing. It's a profound shift to move our awareness from what we are going to say in response to the *quality of receiving* that we are offering our friend, who is taking the risk to open up and share the gift of their inner lives with us. From this perspective, the quality of our listening is more important than the content of any advice we have to offer in reply.

It takes a high level of steadiness and openness to listen to each other this powerfully. When we can hear what someone we love has lived through, and suspend the urge to judge or fix them in the process, their secret truths become invitations to be truly present, right in the middle of all the paradoxes, inconsistencies, traumas, and transformations that every human life contains. This is how deep listening relieves suffering, both for speaker and listener. In this act of giving and receiving, we remember we are not alone.

Like all qualities of radical friendship, compassionate listening is a capacity we are all born with, and it's one we can train to embody even more fully. This chapter offers several ways we can train our awareness to notice where, why, and how we shut down in relationship to our own or someone else's truths, and some reflections on how we can begin opening up again.

OBSTACLES TO LISTENING: THE FOUR CUPS

In the Japanese Zen and Chinese Chan Buddhist traditions, the internal obstacles that block us from listening with open minds and hearts are described in the analogy of the four cups. The theory is that if we find ourselves unable to listen deeply, it often has something to do with the quality of our mind state at that moment. The four basic mind states that make it hard for us to receive each other's truths—the four kinds of cups—are present for all of us from time to time. We name them because the very act of naming our state of mind can pull us out of being caught in it, and into more of a conscious regard for our own inner condition. As with so many teachings of the Buddhadharma, once we identify the obstacle—the condition of our cup—it's so much easier to dissolve it.

As we go through the description of these four patterns of blocked attention, see if there's any of them that you can recognize in your own experience. How does it feel when you're listening from that particular state of mind? How has it felt when you sense someone is listening to you in that way? And finally, what are some strategies you might try the next time you notice yourself slipping into that particular state of mind, so that you can listen more fully and deeply?

The First Cup: Our Cup Is Already Full

When our cup is already full, there's just no room to receive anything else. Another drop, and the contents would spill over the rim. The analogy is meant to describe the state of mind when we aren't really listening to our friend because we believe we already have all the information we need about them and their experience.

Most often, we experience the "full-cup" state of mind with the people who are closest to us. Childhood friends, close colleagues, parents, siblings, roommates—people we know so well that we find ourselves finishing their sentences, whether mentally or out loud. Whenever we hear someone saying *exactly what we thought they would say*, it's a tip-off that we're listening with an already-full cup.

Familiarity, comfort, feeling as if we know someone— these are some of the precious gems of long-term relationships. The only problem is this: the moment we think we already know everything about our friend is the very moment we stop really paying attention to them. And attention is one of the most basic forms of love.

In Zen, "beginner's mind" is the opposite of the full cup. It's the state of awareness when our preconceived ideas about who someone is and what they are going to say are momentarily suspended. With a beginner's mind, we are able to experience each new encounter with minimal baggage from the past. There's space to discover unexpected alignments and surprising connections, precisely because *we know we don't know*, and that not knowing creates the desire to lean in and find out.

Essentially, we empty our cups by meeting our friends (and ourselves) with interest, with the desire to know more that moves us deeper into relationship with one another. A classic way to tap into beginner's mind is to ask ourselves questions that challenge our assumptions and spark our curiosity.

Who is this? we might silently say to ourselves if we find ourselves daydreaming, planning, or otherwise half-listening to someone we know well. Beyond our ordinary way of regarding them, *Who is this, really?* Who are they in this moment? Change is one of the laws of the universe, and we can bet that this person we've known forever is not the same person they were last year, or even last week. (And by the way, neither are we.) Just asking the question *Who is this?* can wake us up from our habitual way of perceiving our friends and help us touch into the truth of impermanence: the uncertainty it brings, and the surprises it reveals.

What's happening right now? We can ask ourselves this question as a way to direct our awareness back into our own present-moment experience. See if you can listen with all your senses—with your ears, with your eyes, with your belly, with your heart. Listen from the back of your body. Listen from the space that surrounds you and your friend. Register vibration, sensation, emotion, as well as the content of what's being shared. Listening with your whole being will help you to be present with what's emerging between you, and to remain present to receive the whole of that gift.

The Second Cup: Our Cup Is Dirty

In the analogy of the dirty cup, our hearts and minds have *space* to receive new information, but that space is covered in residue. So, when our friends try to offer us their truths, their words get smeared with whatever was already in our cup from before. It's a metaphor for the mind that is colored by one of what the Buddha called the "three poisons": greed, hatred, and delusion. These poisons are the core energies that drive our suffering. They can manifest in huge societal ways and in more subtle, personal ones. In the societal sphere, they are akin to what Reverend Dr. Martin Luther King, Jr. called the "three giant triplets" that plague our society: materialism, militarism, and racism. And at the level of our own minds, they are kind of like survival mechanisms that have gotten out of hand, causing us to relentlessly go after what makes us feel good, to destroy what doesn't, and to ignore what we don't understand, no matter the impacts.

Of course, none of us mean to bring these energies into our friendships. When they arise between friends, I think of them more like preexisting conditions. The "dirt" is already there, and it attaches itself to anything that comes into its field of consciousness—including our friends and whatever truths they are trying to share with us. When our minds are like cups that are tinged with greed, they grasp for whatever satisfies our need to be liked and validated. With a mind like this, we hear only what we want to hear, and we are likely to miss whatever words don't fit our desire for confirmation. On the other hand, if our cup is colored with the residue of hatred or aversion, we're likely listening through the lens of judgment or comparison. From this mind state, we hear only what irritates us, what we think is wrong, or what we don't like or agree with, and our interactions with our friends end up snarky. Or, if our minds are like cups that are colored by the third poison, delusion, it can manifest in the quality of our listening as a general fogginess and lack of precision, or even willful ignorance. Everything seems confusing and we don't immediately understand, so we give up trying and mentally check out.

The thing about the three poisons is this: even though they are fundamentally states of mind, when we are truly caught in them, they appear to be coming from somewhere outside of us. For example, if we're in a gathering and find ourselves annoyed by almost everything that anyone says, we might at first believe that we are surrounded by people who are simply the most irritating and offensive people we have ever met. But, it's equally possible that there's a generally aversive mood in our minds, and that we are now seeing everything and everyone through that lens of dislike.

Sometimes, just bringing our attention to the mind state that is blocking us from really listening can start to clear it, like a beam of sunlight dissolves the fog. If we train ourselves to pull our attention away from the object of our irritation (or attachment, or delusion) and instead turn inward to investigate *our own* body sensations, thoughts, and emotions, the state often becomes less believable and less "sticky." That shift from judging others to noticing the source of the judgment, that shift from object to subject, is the radical turn that the mindfulness practices invite us to take.

But, if awareness alone doesn't clear it, and we've already observed everything there is to observe about whatever mental poison is present for us, we may need to apply an antidote to more actively clean our cup.

The antidotes to the three poisons involve cultivating the opposite of whatever our particular state of mind might incline us toward.

- If it's aversion that's preventing us from listening deeply, we can work on developing our love, gratitude, and patience, either through a practice like metta or through embodying the energy of friendliness as gentleness and warmth.
- If it's greed that's causing us to objectify our friends rather than listen to them, the antidote might be allowing the element of space to balance the closing-in, narrowing energy of clinging. We can do that by bringing our attention to the space between us and the person we're hearing, noticing the space between objects, and even the pauses between words as this person speaks to us.
- The deluded mind, that third poison, is hazy and fuzzy and imprecise. We can counter it with rigor and precision—sharpening the details, clarifying the transitions, and bringing energy to connect the dots between the information we're receiving and what we know to be true.

There may be external conditions that originally set off our tendency to attachment, aversion, or delusion. But once internalized, cleaning our cup becomes an inside job. Applying antidotes to clean our cups is about wise response rather than a fixed set of rules. Sometimes, we'll need to bring more softness; other times, we'll need to firm up with more energy. In either case, we'll develop the power to listen more compassionately by recognizing when a preexisting mind state is preventing us from being fully present, and by directly working with that state to restore our natural capacity to receive.

The Third Cup: Our Cup Is Upside Down

When we're listening with a mind like a cup turned upside down, it means we're not listening at all. The shop is closed. No one is home. We've mentally erected a wall between ourselves and another person.

From time to time, turning our cup over and tuning out for the purposes of rest, rejuvenation, and safety can be a wise act of self-preservation. *Especially* if we have been oppressed by society, we most likely haven't always had a choice when it comes to receiving harmful speech about ourselves or people we love.

If, however, we find ourselves listening to someone whose views offend us, but are not directed *at* us, it might be a strategic moment to turn our cup right-side up and listen to what they have to say. *White people, straight people, able-bodied people, men, and others in positions of societal privilege: I'm talking to you.* When you are willing to listen

147

and engage with someone who has confused or harmful views about people who are marginalized by society in ways that you happen not to be, deep listening is a practice of radical friendship toward the folks that person might go on to harm if they *don't* have a safe space to work out their thinking with someone like you, who can listen without putting themselves in harm's way.

It used to be that we stayed away from politics in family gatherings. I don't think we can afford to do that anymore. Change doesn't happen by way of strangers going around knocking on doors, trying to convert people they don't know to a radically different set of views. That kind of transformation of consciousness doesn't typically happen in encounters between strangers. But it *can* happen in the context of loving, committed friendships and other kinds of relationships. The kind of relationships where even if we disagree, we won't desert each other.

So, when Uncle Larry starts making wild generalizations or unfounded assertions at a holiday dinner, think twice about rolling your eyes and changing the subject, or spewing a bunch of facts in his direction. Most likely, you are not getting news from the same sources, and you don't believe each other's sources are credible anyway. Lobbying facts at each other will only leave you locked in a back-and-forth debate.

The only time I've gotten any traction with relatives or family friends who make offensive jokes or express harmful views is when I listen with the genuine intent to understand how they feel, and why. It takes all the skills of clearing a dirty cup—suspending, at least momentarily, my desire to have them see things my way, and my aversion to what they've said—to respond with something like: *Tell me more about why you feel that way.* And then, to relax and let them tell me.

The idea here is to get underneath the layers of intellectual defense and touch the needs and emotions that are driving their beliefs. When I'm able to say, *I can tell you really care about this issue. Can you help me understand why you feel the way you do?* and listen with an open cup, *and* when they're willing to speak from the heart of their own experience, sometimes magic happens in that space. We're no longer boxers, trading jabs from opposite sides of the ring. We're on the same side of humanity, the *only* side, the side that wants to feel safe, be valued, and live full and meaningful lives. We may still have very different views on how we got into the mess we're all in now and how we get out of it. But, at least we've established a common ground and opened the door to future conversations in which we can speak and listen without solidifying each other into right and wrong, hero and enemy.

We all have our limits. Some days, we won't have space to listen compassionately to someone who we feel is spouting nonsense, even if we think we should. And as I said before, if we find ourselves in a position where someone with relatively more privilege is directing harmful speech *toward* us, or someone like us, it is perfectly acceptable to turn over our cups and walk away. But, if we find ourselves on equal footing with "the opposition"—at the family dinner, on the next barstool, or in the airplane seat beside us—and we have a little space that day, maybe we can turn our cup over and listen, even for a bit, and ask questions that lead to more listening.

We may just learn something about what matters to both of us, and find new ways of expressing how we can be *truly* safe, valued, and cared for in this world. And on the right day, without saying anything at all, we may just listen someone into a higher understanding.

The Fourth Cup: Our Cup Has a Hole in It

The cup with a hole in it is a metaphor for what happens when we listen, but don't retain what we hear. New information comes in, but it flows right out, and the next time we go looking for it, it's just not there. We may mean no harm, we may just be prone to forgetting, but when we can't remember something that's important to our friends, they often experience it like we just don't care.

It's natural to feel a little wobbly when it comes to learning unfamiliar concepts that our friends or loved ones introduce to us, or when trying on new behaviors. It's even understandable to feel a little defensive about our seeming inability to retain what we've learned. But that's no reason to give up. When folks take the time to teach us how they want to be addressed or put us on to new language or ideas that matter to them, it's rarely because they're trying to trip us up or shame us. It's because they care enough to let us in. We can return that care by paying attention as best we can and trying again.

The word we usually translate as "mindfulness" in English—*sati* in Pali—means something like "to remember." If we think of remembering someone's name, pronouns, or other needs or preferences as a part of our daily mindfulness practice, it can shake up our habitual patterns of speaking and listening—in a good way. It not only helps prevent verbal missteps in the future but it also changes the way we think about the person. Which is, of course, the point: not to be right, but to start to see others the way they wish to be seen.

When we have a mind like a cup with a hole in it, it's often because our default assumption is that other people think the way we think and want the same things we want. It takes extra effort to remember how different we all are. I remember the first time a friend of many years gave me the feedback that when she's sharing a difficulty she's going through, she needs me to listen differently. My tendency is to say something like, "Ugh, that sucks so much, sounds really hard, you poor thing . . ." Mostly, I realize, because that's the kind of response *I* want when I'm sharing with a friend. I want gooey empathy. I want verbal cuddles. I want my friends to affirm how damn hard it all is.

But *this* friend? She asked if I could skip the cooing and just remind her that she's strong, she's capable, and that she's *got this*. At first, I felt defensive. *Why is my natural way of responding not good enough?* But thankfully, it didn't take me long to realize it had nothing to do with me. My friend was sharing what she needs, and loving her means being willing to listen and respond in a way that's a little foreign to me, a little unnatural, and therefore a little uncomfortable. I tell you, though, trying to do a new thing keeps me on my toes. It requires me to listen and respond from a place of deep intention. Which, ultimately, is where I want to be.

LISTENING AS A SUPERPOWER

When we find ourselves at the limits of our capacity to hear someone we care about, it's not *always* because of an internal obstacle like those described in the analogy of the four cups. It's always worth at least investigating our inner state, because if the source of the blockage is in our own mind, shifting that is a whole lot easier and more effective than trying to shift the world around us. Sometimes though, we find it hard to listen because what we're listening to is truly very hard to be with. As we deepen in friendship with one another, truths that have long been kept secret start to feel safe enough to come out into the open. There can be histories of abuse, assault, and neglect. Struggles with addiction. Profound loss and lingering grief. Structural injustices can intensify these experiences, but even without them, the scope of human suffering can be mind-blowingly overwhelming.

When we listen to each other, it's not just the words we're hearing. It's the energy behind the words that moves us. As we tell our stories, our words weave fields in which others can join us. Other people's stories can resonate with untold secrets from our own lives or our family lines and soften the edges that separate speaker from listener. As listeners, that energy can take us into the past, it can move us across space, and it can strike chords in us that expand our compassion for our friends into a deep reverence for all of life, a kind of awe at the vast fields of sorrows and joys it contains.

In moments when we feel too overwhelmed, when the suffering seems too deep and we've lost sight of our own and each other's resilience, we can build our capacity to listen by asking for help.

A few years back, I was invited by the organization GreenFaith to attend a gathering of young faith leaders from around the world, just before the 2015 United Nations Climate Change Conference in Paris. Our job was to generate a global multi-faith climate justice campaign. We kicked off our convening at a monastery in Rome with presentations by leaders from regions that were being hit hardest by the climate crisis. I listened to firsthand accounts of unprecedented storms, wildfires, droughts, and rising temperatures around the world and saw pictures of the effects on the land, animals, and people—predominantly poor people and people of color. When the climate activist Betty Barkha showed us images of the eroding coastlines in her homeland of Fiji, a result of sea levels rising, she delivered a message from her elders as well: "They told me to ask you to please send earth, send sand," she said through her tears. "What we had is slipping away."

That was when I lost it. I walked out to the bathroom and sobbed in despair. The climate disaster seemed too far gone. I couldn't see our way out of this mess. I felt so far from the center of decision-making, unable to contribute to stopping the crisis in any meaningful way. It had been a long time since I'd prayed. I grew up Catholic, and I'd made my break from the politics of the Church in my early teens. But right there, in the bathroom stall of a Catholic monastery in the heart of Rome, I let my heart whisper: *I need help.*

When I dried my tears and left the bathroom, I saw Yeb Saño, sitting on a bench across the courtyard, looking up at the sky. Yeb was one of the organizers of the convening, a climate delegate from the Philippines who was leading a pilgrimage on foot from Rome to Paris. I sat down next to him and looked out over the yard. "How's it going?" he asked. Fresh tears started rolling down my cheeks. I should have been a lawyer, I told him. Or a researcher, or a politician. Someone who could do something about this rapidly heating planet. He listened to me and then was silent for a while.

"You know what I do when I feel powerless?" he asked. "I ask myself three questions: First: What do I love? What do I love so much that it lights up my heart, that I would protect it with my life? The second question is: What is my skill set? What do I know how to do, and do well? And the third, well, it's not exactly a question. I just think to myself: *no action is too small.* It's a mini pep talk, and while it may not even be true in the ultimate sense, it gets me moving again when I get stuck."

We sat together a while and talked, side by side, about my answers to those questions.

Eventually, Yeb asked if I was ready to go back into the conference. I was.

In the years since, I've used his questions countless times when I feel uncertain about how to respond to the suffering I'm witnessing on large scale.

What do I love? What brings us joy gives us clues about what's really important to us. And engaging in what we love or working on behalf of what and who we love generates a kind of energy that magnetizes resources and helps keep us going in the right direction.

What is my skill set? Considering our skills and unique leverage points for change helps focus our efforts in ways that can yield maximum impact. We are all good at different things, and we need a diversity of strategies to drive change. How can the capacities we have already developed be used in service of what we love and care about?

Can I do something small? It's easy to get stuck in thinking mode when trying to devise an intervention we can make all on our own that will transform society. Often, what we need is to try something out, and learn from the doing of it. Reflecting on your love and your skills, what is the smallest viable action you can take in response to what your community needs? Can you try it today?

Just asking the questions, pausing to listen to whatever answers bubble up in response, has been on numerous occasions enough to move me out of despair and restore my capacity for action.

Yeb pointed me toward a practice of listening more deeply to myself, and to the still, small, wise voice inside me. Since that day, I've used just as often the equally valuable skill of asking the universe for help, which is what I believe led me to sit down next to him and open up in the first place. Sometimes, the universe comes to me in the form of people like Yeb who, when I don't know how to continue listening to the suffering in the world, will pause and listen to the suffering in me. Sometimes, the universe comes to me in the form of a power that exists both within and beyond the human realm. Big, big forces, way bigger than me, that I can lean into for the strength and courage to stay present and keep on listening, even when it's difficult.

Kuan Yin is one of these massive powers. She's a deeply revered deity in Mahayana Buddhist lineages, a Chinese incarnation of the divine feminine, and a figure who appears by different names in different faith traditions. The Buddhist teacher Kittisaro describes her as "a metaphor for the deepest heartbeat of the universe: a heart that is empty yet filled with listening."[29] It's said that she hears all the sounds of the world, and when anyone anywhere calls out to her, she responds. Though much of Western Buddhism has a decidedly secular bent, I've found that including the beings or energies who are bigger than me has given me access to a tremendous amount of support in my practice and life, and to the qualities of humility and surrender that secular mindfulness sometimes lacks.

The spiritual practices of my childhood were filled with ways of calling out to the divine and the confidence that we were being heard. I loved church not for the sermons, but for the incense, the singing, and the standing and sitting down together. For the rhythm of the rituals, formal and informal, that punctuated our Sunday services.

Kuan Yin practices appeal to these parts of me. When I recite mantras that call the various names of Kuan Yin, I let the vibrations of the sound fill my awareness, and channel all the contents of my heart into the sound. The uncertainty and the frustration and the heartbreak. The suffering that rises up from the earth and the genocides it has seen. I imagine that sound like a river from my heart flowing into the heart of a great, compassionate being. Paradoxically, turning it over and letting it flow doesn't make me feel powerless. It is a huge relief to be at the end of my rope and call out the names of the divine. It is a huge blessing to immediately receive the sense that I'm not alone, that the container of my heart has become a little wider and its contents a little lighter.

It's well worth the time it takes to develop a relationship with a being who has a greater capacity for listening than we do, someone or something we can think of and emulate in moments of overload. It could be with a deity like Kuan Yin or a real-life hero or mentor who has inspired us with their ability to be with the sorrow of life and remain buoyant. It could be the ocean, it could be the sky, it could be the force of love in the sum of all human hearts. When we feel like our world is too much for us to handle, we can plug into a force that *is* powerful enough to meet the challenges before us.

All we need is a method for tapping in. It may be a visualization, song, prayer, chant, or some combination of the above. It may mean actually going there—to wade in the water, to lay on the earth, to lean against the mountain, or to gaze at the clouds passing through the sky. When we put our bodies in the position to feel held, supported, and illuminated by something bigger than us, we can sense learn from these qualities, absorb and embody from them.

Our expansiveness as listeners makes us more reliable as friends. Other people trust that we can receive their experiences without becoming overwhelmed or making it all about us. And, we begin to trust ourselves, our capacity to meet our truths, and the truths of this world with compassionate listening and compassionate response.

PRACTICE
Listening Meditation

Sound, like the breath or a mantra, is a classic object for meditation. By attending to the sense of hearing with our awareness and bringing our attention back to sound when it wavers, our minds can't help but become more settled over time. Meditation on sound tends to create an expansive, receptive kind of mind. Meditating on sound is also said to be Kuan Yin's preferred meditation practice. One of the names she goes by is "She Who Listens at Ease to the Sounds of the World."

To engage in this practice, first, find your comfortable meditation posture. Let your hands rest and your eyes close or softly open to the space in front of you, not looking at anything in particular, just resting.

Check in with yourself to acknowledge your inner landscape and what you're bringing to the practice. If you discover any difficulty, distraction, or stress, take it as an opportunity to be extra kind to yourself.

Now, turn your awareness to the sense-gate of your ears. Notice any sound vibrations that are currently making contact with your eardrums. Let your ears be like wide open satellite dishes, receiving all sounds near and far away Some ambient sounds may seem more constant. Others arise and pass quickly within the field of awareness. Notice that sometimes the mind will follow after one particular sound, often one that we find especially pleasant or unpleasant. Or, we can slide from *hearing* sound into *thinking about* the sound: where it's coming from, and why, and what it means. When this happens, see if it's possible to bring your attention back to the wide-open simplicity of hearing and awareness of all the sounds, without holding on or pushing away sound, if you can.

Using sound as your anchor or home base for attention yields a quality of awareness that is different from the quality of awareness we experience when we pay attention to the breath or other body sensations. How would you describe the difference? What Kuan Yin–like qualities do you witness arising in you with the development of this practice?

(7)

Don't Abandon

Monks, a friend endowed with [this]
quality is worth associating with. . . .
When misfortune strikes, they will
not abandon you.

—*Mitta Sutta*

THE EPIC STORY of the Buddha's enlightenment began
when he left home in search of truth and freedom. It's
the tradition we call "going forth"—leaving behind family,
friends, and the comfort of the known world in search of
freedom, destiny, and purpose. It's the pursuit of something greater.

I've often wondered how stories like these have influ-
enced those of us who practice in the many spiritual traditions that hold the act of leaving home as a spiritual ideal.
In beautiful ways, going forth is a willingness to journey
beyond, a passion for discovery, an adventurous spirit. And
in not-so-beautiful ways, it's restless wanderlust, a distaste
for the mundane world, and the sense that the holy life is
always "somewhere else."

We can think of the sixth quality of spiritual friendship that the Buddha describes, the quality of "not abandoning each other," as loyalty: the capacity to stay. Loyalty helps us to build relationships by giving them the commitment they need to deepen, solidify, and grow. At the collective level, there's no organization, community, or social movement that can survive without a critical mass of people who stay committed to them over the long haul. When we stay with a cause that we care about, we help it to build the mass and momentum it needs to make an impact. The same is true with our friendships. It's a blessing to make new friends as we move and change. And, there's just something about being with people who have known us since we had frizzy hair and wore our pants too high.

For freedom-loving people, learning to stay can be a bit of a challenge. I know that's true for me. For years, I feared getting stuck in a relationship or a community that eventually wouldn't work for me anymore and not being able to get out. So, I mostly drifted, dipping in to connect, but not staying so long that I could get sucked in. What I missed was the possibility of friendships and community relationships as we navigate change and stay together.

What I've learned since is that true loyalty has freedom in it. It doesn't mean being locked down for our whole lives. Knowing that we are free to go, and knowing how and when to go when we need to, can give us the confidence we need to choose to stay—in friendship and in community. This chapter is a celebration of both of these qualities: the loyalty we offer to others through their inevitable ups and downs, and the commitment not to abandon ourselves in the process.

WHEN MISFORTUNE STRIKES

So, what does the *Mitta Sutta* mean by "When misfortune strikes, they [the friend] won't abandon you"? As individuals, we can experience misfortunes like shaky finances, sickness, injuries, or a mental/emotional challenge like anxiety or depression. Within relationships, misfortunes can take the shape of misunderstandings, misalignments, betrayals—the kinds of friction and breakdowns that happen in the spaces between us. And in communities and organizations, we can experience misfortunes like unexpected changes in leadership, scandals, abuse, as well as the impacts of outside forces beyond our control. Because our individual, relational well-being, and collective well-being aren't actually separate, misfortunes typically span multiple domains at once.

The sutta states that when any of these kinds of misfortunes strike, the true friend will not abandon you. This is significant because usually when we witness misfortune, our default response as human beings is to back up and turn away, as if poverty, heartbreak, or other hard times might be contagious. It is such a subtle and habitual reaction that we may not even know we're doing it until we pay attention. The fear of contagion exists even in our relationship with the suffering of our own hearts. We tend to compartmentalize the parts of ourselves that have experienced pain and misfortune. We don't want to look for fear that looking will make it real, make it spread. But of course, we know in our heart of hearts that looking away takes its toll on our souls.

When we turn toward misfortune instead of away, when we open to the suffering that misfortunes cause with love, what naturally arises is the boundless, divine, radiant state of heart and mind known as compassion. It is a blossoming of our hearts that *only* happens in response to our own and others' suffering. For me, understanding the interrelatedness of suffering and compassion has changed how I feel about misfortune in general. Instead of seeing suffering as something to be avoided at all costs (as if that were possible), we can recognize suffering as an inevitable part of our human experience that offers us the opportunity to expand the range of our hearts. Not abandoning ourselves or each other when we are hurting, and being willing to accompany each other even in hard times, is a capacity of true friendship that we can cultivate through our practice.

LOYALTY TO SENSATION

Mindfulness of the body is a beautiful practice for cultivating loyalty, the quality we need to stay in relationship even through ups and downs. When we practice awareness of breath or body, our loyalty is to sensation itself. The practice is to stay with the sensations even as they change.

Mindfulness isn't a thought. It's a full-bodied sensory experience. The language of the body is sensation, and feeling is the way we listen. Showing up for the pulsing and tingling, the numbness, the heat, the heaviness, the expansiveness, and all the rest of it is a way of embodying loyalty at the most granular level.

Feel the moment when a new breath enters the nostrils. Cool, maybe a bit dry. The chest rises, a sense of fullness. The sensation of the spine rocking forward slightly. The back ribs expanding, the belly extending, and the throat opening. Lightness, space, length, pressure—and then, in an instant, the inhalation turns. Breathing out, feel the warmth of the exhalation. Just a thin stream at first, and then a rush. Softening, deepening, emptying out. A pause before the lungs open up again.

At Spirit Rock Meditation Center, on the unceded Ohlone territory known as Woodacre, California, there's a gratitude hut that is filled with pictures of revered teachers and bits of wisdom from their teachings. Under a photograph of the Thai meditation master Ajahn Mun are these words from him: "In your investigation of the world, never let the mind desert the body."

I can't imagine that any of us *intend* to desert our bodies. But while developing a meditation practice, many of us discover that we've partially evacuated our bodies somewhere along the way. Traumatic experiences stored in the tissues of the body can make it feel like an unsafe place. Our bodies may have been subjected to impossible standards of beauty, desexualized, oversexualized, or pathologized in the gaze of the dominant culture. As we pay attention to the dance of sensation across the field of our awareness from moment to moment, fear and sadness sometimes present themselves to be known and healed—whether or not we have invited them.

Our bodies are innocent. They want to be as healthy, happy, and whole as they can be. They want to expand into the fullest expressions of themselves. They want to be free, unencumbered by judgments, restrictions, and impossible standards. And if we turn away from them, overwhelmed by the multitudes they contain, we will miss the wisdom they have to share with us about how freedom happens at the cellular level, at the level of muscle and bone. They won't talk to us at all unless we love them enough not to leave when they start to tell us their stories.

We can make friends with our bodies by approaching them with gentleness. With our loyal awareness, we can demonstrate our commitment to our somatic experiences. By paying attention moment by moment, it is as if we are saying to our bodies: *I'm not going to abandon you. For this period of time that I'm practicing mindfulness of body, you can be however you need to be, and I'm going to stay right here with you, no matter what. I won't judge you. I won't compare you to how you used to be, and I sure won't make plans to fix you. If you have something to say, I'll listen. If you don't, I'll still be right here.*

Our bodies receive our attention as love, and under the soft glow of loving awareness, knots start to unwind and deep holdings start to release. *We* don't do it—the body does it on its own. And the body has its own timing, so it will take as long as it takes.

If we find that when we return our attention to the body there's a lot of intense sensation, resistance, or fear, we can start with just one minute of practicing this way. One minute of bringing awareness to bodily or breath sensations, and then moving our attention to something outside our bodies that feels less activating and more concrete: the ground, the sky, a flower blooming. Our practice then is to come back when we can and, over time, stay a little longer when we are able.

It's amazing how much can be revealed through this simple practice of loyalty by feeling whatever is unfolding *right now*, and learning to stay with it, moment after moment. In the process, we become more gathered, collected, and sure in our ability to meet whatever arises internally without flinching or turning away. Nurtured by unwavering commitment, the body learns that it can trust the mind and heart, and we can walk in the world with unconditional confidence, the foundation of which is love.

GOOD-ENOUGH COMMUNITY

The theory of the "good-enough" parent emerged in the early 1950s when British pediatrician Donald Winnicott observed several different parenting styles and their impacts on the children he saw as patients. He noticed that when a parent failed to meet their child's every need, it was *beneficial* for the child's development. As long as the disappointments were small and manageable, they served as valuable catalysts for the child to learn how to tolerate discomfort and soothe themselves. When a parent isn't always available but is "good enough," the child learns they are not the center of the universe, that they can be bored or disappointed or not get their way and still be OK. In this way, the good-enough parent is the perfect parent because they prepare their child to live in a world where they are not always in control.

Lately, I've been thinking about what constitutes a good-enough *community*. The story I used to tell myself was that I was a loner, not fitting in anywhere in particular. It's true for all of us on some level—a single community can never encompass all of who we are. There's an inherent dissatisfaction in that fact, and my solution was to hang out on the edges of communities rather than getting into the middle of them. I was a dancer and performer, but I thought other dancers were dramatic and self-centered. I was an activist who thought activists were all transaction and no chill. I was a dedicated practitioner of Buddhism who could hardly stand other Buddhists—pretentious, aloof, and overly academic, I thought. Can you say, *judgmental*? But for me, judgment was a protective measure. As an observer, I could dip in when I felt like it, skip out if things got messy, and hope that no one would notice or care much either way.

What I couldn't see at the time was that the flaws I fixated on in communities—dramatic, self-centered, transactional, no chill, pretentious, aloof, and overly academic—were also qualities that lived in me, and I privately gave myself hell for. It was not until I finally got off the sidelines and got all the way in to the communities that I had circled around that I confronted *my own* feelings of not good enough. If I didn't fully commit to a group of friends or community of practice, I was safe from people seeing *all* of me—the stuff I'm not proud of, the stuff I'm still working out.

The first flush of interest in a new friend, organization, or community is a lot like falling in love. There's this feeling of *Yes, I've finally found The One!* It always takes a little more time for the cracks and rough edges to show. A momentary lack of consideration. A last-minute cancellation. A unilateral decision without checking in. I'll admit, my first instinct when I see a mistake (or make a mistake) is to run like the dickens. I don't want to stick around for what may be only the tip of an iceberg of unskillful behavior. And I don't want to face being rejected when my new friends realize that *I'm* sometimes anxious, sometimes late, and that I sometimes take on more than I can actually handle.

Belonging is rarely discovery. It's a decision. If we experience the disappointment that people and communities will never be perfect, and we stay friends anyway, something sacred happens in that place. If there is enough good for us to stay, we teach each other that we are worth staying *with*. If we truly accept rupture as a natural part of what groups do together, then when it happens, we may still be disappointed, but we won't be surprised, and we won't abandon ship. We'll engage our wise speech and compassionate listening to seek out what's on the other side of that rupture. When we're lucky, we'll find repair, resolution, and an opportunity to begin again.

The best thing about being good enough is that we don't have to get ourselves 100 percent together to be available for radical friendship. Rather, it is through the practice of friendship that we get ourselves together. It takes courage to commit, and it takes wisdom to know what good enough is—and what it is not.

TRUSTING THE PRINCIPAL WITNESS

So, how do we know whether to stay or go? For those of us who have been marginalized by society in some way, this question can be especially confusing. Institutions have taught us that our assessments about the world and ourselves are incorrect, that we can't be trusted, we won't be believed. As a result, we tend to second-guess what we see and feel.

There's a phrase from the *lojong* mind-training slogans that I often call on in moments of doubt. Lojong is a series of essential Mahayana Buddhist teachings that were distilled into slogans by the Tibetan luminary Chekawa Yeshe Dorje in the twelfth century. This is my favorite:

Of the two witnesses, trust the principal one.

The two witnesses the slogan refers to are (1) ourselves and (2) other people. Our own perspective is the principal one. This is not to say that we should ignore feedback and outside opinions. It's to say that if we are practicing well, cultivating love, and listening to and learning about ourselves and each other—if we are doing the good work of radical friendship—then we can begin to trust our felt sense of things. And, we don't always have to rely on the opinions of other people to know what to do. We can begin to trust our own perception and hold it in the highest regard.

Some of the commitment-phobia I experienced earlier in my life was rooted in the fear that once I got into friendships or relationships with communities, I wouldn't be able to get out. As I began to say yes to more roles in service and leadership, I discovered that this was completely true. It wasn't just that I had no exit skills. It was also that, deep down, I believed that I *owed* my loyalty to every individual and institution that had ever been kind to me. Once committed, I didn't think I had the right to leave. I experienced a clap of doubt when there was a discrepancy between how I felt and what others told me I *should* feel or what *they* felt. So, I stayed in "friendships" with people who I could tell didn't even like me. I stayed at jobs where I was undervalued and underpaid and in organizations I knew weren't being true to their missions. I stayed in romantic relationships that had long since lost their joy. I didn't trust my ability to assess whether these situations were worth being loyal to, so I made my decisions according to other people's desires and demands. Out of fear of abandoning others, I abandoned myself.

When we make others the principal witnesses of our lives, when we trust their assessments more than our own, there's often something in it for us too. Putting others' opinions first relieves us of the responsibility of making our own decisions. Staying in relationships with people or organizations who drain us may be exhausting, but at least we get to feel needed. Sometimes, we give our power away because we have the sense that our power is so enormous. We have so much love, so much clarity, and so much deep wisdom that we don't even know what to do with it all, and we end up selling it for cheap.

I began this section with a contemplation on loyalty to sensations because embodied knowing is cellular, bone-deep. When we pay attention to how our bodies feel in the presence of others, it gives us important information about the relationship. Are we feeling warmth, ease, relaxation, and openness in the presence of our friends? Is there a sense of tension, holding, or bracing when we are in conversation? Do we feel there is enough space for us, or is there a feeling of holding back or fighting for room? It's healthy to have some degree of creative tension in friendships. If we carry a lot of privilege, a little challenge can be healing for the parts of us that believe we are entitled to comfort at all times. But, if the most consistent embodied experience in a particular relationship is one of struggle, that's data we shouldn't ignore. And, if we've experienced more than our share of challenges of just living in an unjust world, we really need at least some of our friendships and communities to be spaces of refuge and ease, where our bodies can actually relax. Where we can breathe deeply, laugh well, love, and be loved in extraordinary measure.

When we are in a relationship that doesn't feel balanced, we can first ask ourselves, *Is there a way I can stay in relationship with this person or group, and be in it differently?*

There's a wide field of possibility between staying and going, and there's deep spiritual practice there. When we change the way we participate in a relationship or community, everything else shifts too. If we've been doing too much and we pull back, we make space for other people to move forward and into their own agency. We are the cocreators of our friendships. When something's not working, we have the opportunity to see how we've contributed to the problem and to see if changing our contribution can be part of the solution.

Another practice that can help us assess if the conditions are right to stay is the practice of *naming*—saying out loud exactly what you're observing in yourself and in the relationship. If you're anything like me, you may feel that you can't name an experience you're having unless you have it 100 percent figured out—especially not if you're the first to speak up about it. This is crap. It's totally valid to simply name that something feels off to you, and that you'd like to explore it together. If we're feeling uncomfortable or witnessing unacceptable behavior and we speak up about it, we can bring it into our shared awareness and have the opportunity to collectively rise to a higher standard.

That's the difference between abandonment and letting go. Radical friendship means we don't leave each other at the first glimpse of imperfection or hint of conflict. It also means we don't stay in relationships and organizations that require us to abandon ourselves. Even friendships that have been beautiful and healing sometimes change.

Bottom line? We don't need anybody's permission to let go of a relationship that doesn't support our liberation. Other people may not agree, which is why trusting the principal witness is so important. There *is* a part of us that knows. We can intuitively know when a friendship is no longer a true one, and when it's time to dissolve it. If we must walk away, we can truly say we did everything we could and remained loyal to our own experience.

Right now, my favorite community of practice is one that has no name and cannot be found on any website. It's a group of five women who meet on Thursday nights, via video chat, to articulate a spiritual practice that uplifts the power of the divine feminine. We started as a month-long book club, and we stayed because we enrich each other's lives. We're all Buddhists, but it's not *all* that we are—we are also healers, parents, witches, writers, tarot readers, and wide-traveling seekers. Each of us was having trouble finding the community we wanted so we made one up—a tiny one, where we can express our inner lives, interests, and dreams in vivid emotional tones that resonate, jewel-like, between us.

I didn't quit the more established communities I'm a part of, but this is the one that feels like my truest spiritual home right now, the one that gives me the creative space to stay a part of the others. Lineage, authenticity, and tradition are so important, but they are no more important than innovation, adaptation, and creating new portals to tap into universal truths.

My Thursday-night sisters circle developed out of nothing, will persist as long as we wish to participate in it, and can dissolve back into nothing once it's served its purpose. I understand less and less why institutions fight to survive past their relevance to those they serve. There's no effervescence for me in organizations that keep going just because they've been *going all this time*. I'd rather the communities I'm a part of live on in stories of what we've created together, on the tongues of the people who've loved us and who've been touched by the waves we've made.

PRACTICE

Tonglen

Tonglen is a meditation practice that comes from Tibetan Buddhism. It means "sending and taking." In many ways, it's the exact opposite of New-Agey practices where we breathe in the light and breathe out the darkness. In tonglen, we take in any obstruction, blockage, or stuckness that exists in our own hearts or anywhere around us. We transform this obstruction inside our hearts and send out clarity, openness, spaciousness, and ease. It's a training that can help transform our fear of misfortune, to stay with it long enough to transform it.

From the Buddhist perspective, there is no truly bad energy that we are inhaling. What we are breathing in is our *concept* of bad energy, our fear of contagion, or habitual mental patterns that are between us and opening to our own and others' suffering. We start to reroute our conditioning, turning away by turning toward and breathing it in. Using these concepts and visualizing sending and taking with each breath, we start to build confidence that we don't have to fear difficulty; we can meet it with compassion.

Begin the practice by just connecting with your breath or bodily sensations for a while to ground and relax you a bit.

When you feel somewhat settled, start imagining that when you breathe in, you are breathing in thick, gray smoke. Imagine that the smoke is purified by your heart and lungs, so when you breathe out, you breathe out sunshine and fresh air. Repeat this for a few minutes with an easy, relaxed breath, not straining too much, just letting your breath come and go as you visualize the smoke being transformed into fresh air.

Now, check in with your heart. Feel the sensations that are present in that space. Notice any emotions or moods that are there. Open, to whatever degree possible, to any heartache that may linger there. Feelings of disappointment, betrayal, or hopelessness—sense any resistance to these emotions you may encounter, any way you may be struggling to keep them out. On your next in-breath, breathe in the emotions, imagining them riding in on the thick, gray smoke. As you breathe out, breathe out clarity and ease into your own heart, and imagine fresh air that is infusing the space where heartache lived before. Keep going like this for a few minutes, breathing in the smoke of your personal experience and breathing out spaciousness and peace.

As you continue your breathing, consider all the other

beings who may be experiencing a similar kind of heart-break at this very moment. While no one on the planet has had your exact experience, many have gone through similar struggles and feel a similar kind of pain. Let all your awareness reach out to all those people right now, all over the world. The next time you breathe in, breathe in whatever it is that weighs on not just your heart, but all the hearts that also know the pain you feel; draw it in like thick, gray smoke filling your lungs. As you breathe out, breathe out sparkling clean, bright air to all the beings who are going through something like what you're going through. Repeat this pattern for a few minutes as you take and send to this group of people like you.

Now consider all the people in the world who suffer in ways you haven't directly experienced. See if you can connect with the sense that while you may be very different in some ways, you can be sure that, just like you, they want to be happy and not suffer too. So, the next time you breathe in, imagine that you are breathing in all the heartbreak and suffering in the whole wide world in order to transform it with your great big heart. As you breathe out, breathe out enough spaciousness and brightness for the whole world to feel relief from what hurts. Do this for a few rounds of breath.

Finally, imagine that through your efforts, just for a few moments, every obstruction in the world has been removed. Breathe clear air in and out, feel the experience of freedom that is also always there, sometimes as close as our next breath.

PRACTICE

Writing the Community Ideal

The next time you have some time to spare after your meditation practice, take a few moments to envision and feel into your good-enough community.

- How does it feel in your body when you imagine being a part of this group?
- What kind of emotions or moods do you notice in your heart or mind?
- What parts of yourself are being seen and celebrated?
- What are you learning?
- How are you contributing to the well-being of all?

Write your answers down and let this be a living document. Use it periodically to reflect on your relationships with groups, be they colleagues, clubs, political or spiritual homes, or longtime friends who still love to hang out together.

(8)

Don't Look Down

Monks, a friend endowed with [this]
quality is worth associating with . . .
When you're down and out, they
won't look down on you.

—*Mitta Sutta*

THE IDEA BEHIND *bodhicitta*, often translated as "basic goodness," is that all human beings come into this world with
the seed of enlightenment in their hearts. Our lifelong
path of practicing being human is to nurture that seed into
blossoming. In the practice of radical friendship, our path
is to water and nurture these seeds in each other.

We are all in various stages of waking up to our true
nature and healing from whatever obscures it, and some of
these stages are not especially cute. They can be a lot like
school photos from third grade, when we were still figuring
out our hair and clothes and made some regrettable choices
on picture day. But the teachings on bodhicitta remind
us that no matter how messy or ill-fitting our life choices

are at any given moment, at our core, every one of us is fundamentally wise and loving, no matter what. That part of us can never be taken away, and our longtime friends will say we were always beautiful to them, unibrow and all.

When I first learned about the concept of bodhicitta in Buddhism, it rubbed against a deeply held belief I didn't even know I had: some people are essentially bad. The history of the last several thousand years of human existence reads like an extended account of one group of people dominating another, exploiting them and extracting their resources until the next empire came along. Looking at these cycles of violence, it's easy to conclude that some people are inherently greedy, hateful, and deluded. Looking down on colonizers, terrorists, and oppressors makes sense, as long as you can be sure that *those* people are nothing like you and *your* people.

But, even a casual look back into almost any of our family histories reveals a lot more complexity than the dualities of good and bad, oppressor and oppressed, or victim and perpetrator make space for. We all come from people who have been kind, generous, and selfless, enduring tremendous personal sacrifices and even risking their lives to help other people. Most of us also come from people who have used their power over others in ways that have caused tremendous harm. When we have been betrayed, manipulated, or oppressed in some way, we often protect ourselves by creating an "us" and a "them," imagining a fundamental difference between those who harm and those who get harmed. It would be so much easier if that were true, if we could reliably predict based on social location who we can trust, and who is likely to hurt us.

But, I can't tell you how many times I've been unpleasantly surprised by the words or actions of someone who I thought of as "my people" because of what they looked like, or the words they used, or where they were from. When we imagine that people who cause harm fit a particular profile, when we make them "other" and look down on them, we forget their many dimensions, complex histories, and inviolable hearts. If we do, then when *we* are the ones who cause harm, as we all eventually will be, and we are more apt to forget our own humanity as well.

The last instruction on spiritual friendship from the *Mitta Sutta*—not to look down on each other—is an invitation to keep our eyes on each other's bodhicitta, the part of us that is always awake. As radical friends, people who are committed to our own and each other's liberation, we must remember that even when someone commits an act of harm, their innate worthiness is never erased.

I once heard Mariame Kaba, a prison abolitionist and transformative justice practitioner, say, "No one enters violence for the first time by committing it."[30] Her words helped me begin to reconcile my confidence in the basic goodness of all beings with my questions about what in some traditions might be called the existence of evil. There's not always a neat explanation for why people cause harm. It does seem though that people who have been abused—in this lifetime or in previous generations, directly or indirectly—are much more likely to perpetuate abuse.

Not because they are bad, but because they are caught in a powerful cycle of cause and effect that takes a lot of love, intention, and support to disrupt.

Our role as radical friends can be to maintain the view that, underneath it all, there is always a fundamental goodness in each of us. We can prevent or interrupt harm whenever we can without losing sight of that goodness; we can enact boundaries to protect that goodness. We can try our best to connect with and speak to that place of awakening in each other, even if one of us has forgotten who we really are. When we speak to that place of innate goodness in ourselves and in each other, we help bring it forth.

This existence of bodhicitta doesn't mean that we live in a perfect world. It means that this sometimes-messed-up world is perhaps the perfect place to perfect our love. It may be a leap of faith, but it's one that can allow us to show up as the true spiritual friends that we wish to be in this world, only if we are willing to take the risk.

NO LOST CAUSES

The story of Angulimala is one of the most often told about the monks who lived during the Buddha's time. As a child, Angulimala's name was Ahimsaka, which means "harmless one." He was a bright, strong, and gentle boy, and when he grew up, his family sent him to a prestigious university in India. He was so bright that his classmates felt threatened and became jealous of his close relationship with a respected professor. They created an elaborate plan to convince the professor that Ahimsaka had plans to kill and overthrow him. In time, the professor came to believe them.

When Ahimsaka finally completed his degree and was prepared to go home, the professor called him back and told him he had one last task to complete: Ahimsaka would have to make a ceremonial offering of one thousand human fingers to receive credit for his years of study. The professor hoped that Ahimsaka himself would be killed while completing this final assignment, and that his own life would be spared as a result.

At first, Ahimsaka refused. But, faced with the possibility of losing everything he had worked so hard for, he eventually changed his mind. He spent his days in a thick forest, hunting for lone travelers. He went out at night to kill people as they slept in their beds. And he began accumulating piles of little fingers. He strung the fingers together, hung them around his neck, and became known as Angulimala, or "garland of fingers."

On the day that he had accumulated 999 fingers and was looking for one last kill to complete his quota, Angulimala saw his mother enter the forest. She was the only person from his former life who hadn't given up on him, and she had come looking for him against all advice from her friends and family. Angulimala decided to make her little finger his last. He crept up behind her with his sword drawn.

As the story goes, the Buddha appeared on the forest road at that moment between Angulimala and his mother. In his robes and with bare feet, the Buddha slowly walked the road in meditation, looking for all the world like the easiest of marks. Angulimala decided that the Buddha was a better target, but as he went after him, he found that he couldn't catch up. He began to run after him as fast as he could, and though the Buddha was still walking slowly, Angulimala fell farther and farther behind. In exhaustion and desperation, Angulimala screamed at the top of his lungs in the Buddha's direction, arms outstretched. "*Stop!*" he wailed. "*Stop! Stop!*"

The Buddha turned. Though he spoke softly, his voice reverberated from every tree and rock in the forest and from the earth itself, booming in Angulimala's ears. "I have stopped, Angulimala," he said. "Now. *You stop.*"

The Buddha's words shattered Angulimala's trance. He woke up from his obsession. When he came to, and realized what he had been doing all this time, he dropped his sword. Angulimala asked to become one of the Buddha's followers, and the Buddha agreed.

Needless to say, the Buddha's community wasn't exactly thrilled when he brought home a freshly reformed serial killer to be their new roommate. They tried to cast him out, and they excluded him from their conversations and activities whenever they could get away with it. The townspeople who they relied on for food tried to starve him, and sometimes they beat him up, still traumatized from his reign of terror over them. But Angulimala stuck around, stuck with his practice, and never struck back. He endured the karmic results of his prior actions. Eventually, he was said to have become a fully enlightened being, albeit one with a past.

Killing is an extreme example of causing harm, but it's certainly not the only kind. There's a whole spectrum of emotional violence—judging, criticizing, comparing, gossiping, ignoring, and so on—we can commit even against people we call our friends. These moments of subtle harm generate a kind of momentum, and it's possible to be caught in a pattern of behavior so unconsciously and for so long that we don't even notice it anymore. While Angulimala's story is a bit dramatic, his example teaches us that it's always possible to stop—even in the middle of an action, a sentence, a word. No matter how much harm we have caused in the past, with awareness, intention, and effort, we can always change.

When I look back at the harms I've committed in friendships, the biggest aren't the things that I've done, but the things I *haven't* done. I once saw a former roommate walking down the street, and I was so embarrassed I almost ducked into a nearby shop. We'd been great friends before we lived together, but I knew I'd been a crappy roommate. I snacked on her groceries and didn't replace them. My out-of-town guests spent weeks sleeping on our couch. I let dishes pile up in the sink and left my soggy towels on the bathroom floor. Throughout the time we lived together, my roommate went from sitting on the edge of my bed for chats about love and politics to delivering terse greetings through pursed lips on her way in and out of the house. I just let our relationship grow more awkward until about six months in when I suddenly announced I'd be moving to my own place. I hadn't seen or talked to her since the day I moved out.

Several years later, standing there on the street, my old roommate looked genuinely happy to see me. I was happy to see her too, even with all the shame I felt about what a difficult person I'd been to live with. I blurted out an apology for the groceries, the guests, the mess. I hadn't been in a great place mentally or emotionally, I explained. I was having a hard time taking care of myself and our space, and I wished I'd talked to her about it rather than ignoring her obvious frustration.

What I expected was that she would agree I had been a shit person, but that I now appeared to be slightly less of a shit. What she actually said was that she didn't even remember most of the things I apologized for. She just missed me. She was sad that I'd disappeared from her life. Yeah, she admitted, we'd had a shitty six months, but she still loved me. Not keeping in touch after I moved out hurt more than any lack of consideration I'd shown while we lived together.

When we've hurt someone, one of the most radical actions we can take is to acknowledge and apologize for our behavior. It takes a lot of humility to do this, in the true sense of its root word: *humus*, meaning "soil, earth." The same root as the word *human*. To acknowledge that we've done something we wish we hadn't is to acknowledge ourselves to be regular old human beings who make mistakes just like everyone else—who have enough confidence in our fundamental goodness to be OK with admitting it. In a world where the people and forces that hurt us rarely admit responsibility for their actions, just acknowledging that we did something that caused harm can be a deeply healing act of radical friendship.

As important as genuine apologies are, truly making things right with our friends after we've harmed them means more than saying we're sorry. It means changing our behavior. My roommate didn't want to be paid back for the groceries I ate. What she wanted was for me to keep in touch. And for me, that request was astronomically more difficult than settling a tab.

It wasn't the first time I'd heard that I'd hurt someone by fading out of a relationship instead of tackling a difficult conversation head-on. Somehow though, it was the first time I saw how my lack of communication not only caused harm but also kept me from experiencing lasting friendships. I could spend a lot of time looking for new friends every time I felt like I'd messed up with an old one and had to abandon ship. But if I did, then I would never experience the true intimacy of knowing a friend has seen me at my worst and discovering that they'd never lost sight of my best.

Without confidence in our own bodhicitta, it's excruciatingly difficult to acknowledge, apologize, or make amends for the ways we've caused harm in a loving and balanced way. If we feel there is something fundamentally wrong with us, it can simply make us too vulnerable to admit we've done something wrong. Admitting error or fault under those circumstances can threaten what little self-esteem we have and make us feel we are not worthy of true friendship at all. Or, it could go to the other extreme, where our shame drives us to become overly responsible for everything under the sun. Our entire existence becomes an apology, and the people we're in relationships with lose the opportunity to take responsibility for their own behavior when appropriate.

The awakened heart of bodhicitta allows us to admit we've made mistakes without feeling we *are* mistakes. It's vitally important for us to remember our innate goodness when we've caused harm so that we don't look down on ourselves. It's a way of demonstrating radical friendship with our minds and hearts, a way of acting on our worthiness and the innate value that is who we really are.

WHEN WE'VE BEEN HARMED

Hurts need care to heal. But when we've been harmed in a friendship, giving ourselves the care we need—or asking for it from the people we need it from—can be surprisingly hard to do. One of my best friends told me that in the neighborhood where he grew up, if someone took advantage of you, it was considered to be your own fault. You should have seen it coming, and if you didn't, whatever harm you experienced was on you.

In an unjust world, some harms don't even register as harms—it's just the way things are. As a meditation teacher, I've often witnessed how difficult it is for those of us who grew up around a lot of violence—whether physical or psychic, interpersonal or institutional—to even *recognize* when something has hurt us, let alone to admit it to other people. We can become numb to our own pain, or look down on ourselves for being hurt in the first place. Acknowledging we've been harmed by someone we trusted can make us feel that we were wrong to trust them in the first place, or that people *in general* can't be trusted. Or, we can blame ourselves if it feels easier to take on the feeling of being at fault than the feeling of having been wronged by someone else.

True compassion can only arise in a relationship between equals. If we are looking down on ourselves or somebody else who is experiencing suffering, that's not compassion. It's pity. True compassion never loses sight of our own or others' inherent capacity to meet the circumstances of our lives when we have the appropriate support. If we're lucky, our friendships can provide the space and time we need to recognize the wounds we carry, to be supported into our own resilience, and to reflect on our experience in a way that leads to emotional integration and spiritual growth.

A few years ago, I called my mom on the anniversary of Tamir Rice's tragic death. As you probably remember, Tamir was a twelve-year-old Black child who had been playing with a toy gun outside a recreation center in Ohio. A white police officer, Timothy Loehmann, fatally shot him within two seconds of arriving on the scene. Loehmann was fired from his job, not for having killed an innocent child, but for having lied on his job application. He was never charged with a crime of any kind though, and was later hired to work as a police officer again for another Ohio town.

Because my mom had recently moved to Ohio, a few hours drive from where Rice was killed, I asked if she had plans to attend a memorial that day to celebrate his life and to protest how African American communities were being terrorized by the police. She wasn't attending any marches, she said, but she did remember Tamir. She thanked me for reminding her of the anniversary. His death had made her very, very sad, and she wasn't quite sure what to do about it.

"Hey, Katie," she began, shifting the subject a little. "I was reading this interview with the Obamas, and they were discussing what it was like to have 'The Talk' with their daughters. Did you know about 'The Talk?' It's um . . . this talk that Black parents have with their children to prepare them for encountering racism."

I laughed. "Yes, Mom. I know about 'The Talk.'"

"Well," she said. "I don't think I ever gave you all that talk. I guess . . ." She hesitated for a moment and then continued, "I guess you guys learned about racism on your own?"

I thought of myself and my siblings. I nodded and pressed the phone to my cheek. "Yeah," I said. "We did." My mind scrolled through the countless racist incidents I had experienced in my life and never mentioned to her.

"I'm sorry, sweetie. I'm sorry I didn't have 'The Talk' with you. I didn't know I needed to."

I always knew my mom loved us and thought we were beautiful, smart, and incredible human beings. Our family photo was the first thing you saw when you walked into her office, hanging on the wall behind her desk. Four shining brown faces surrounding hers. Strangers sometimes told her how amazing she was to have adopted all four of us together. She would laugh. "Oh, *no*. I'd never adopt four kids. These are *my* babies!" she'd proclaim as she looked at us adoringly.

It wasn't until my mom apologized for *not* preparing me for the inevitable experience of racism that I realized how much the absence of that discussion had hurt. It wasn't just the experiences of racism that I was still healing from. It was also the loneliness of feeling unwelcome to share those experiences with my mom, the person that my young self loved and trusted more than anyone in this world.

I definitely did figure a lot of things out on my own, and this "I'll figure it out myself" mentality created a great deal of self-sufficiency, for which I'm grateful. It also ingrained the stubborn belief that people who don't share my identity not only aren't *interested* in the details of my experience in the world, but they also aren't *capable* of understanding them. Even the people who love me the most.

My mother's apology was a catalyst for me. I didn't ask for it, I didn't expect it, and I didn't even know how much I needed it until she offered it to me. The fact that it came unprompted shook up the assumptions I'd made about her capacity from my earliest experiences trying to talk to her about race. Namely, she would never get it. That apology didn't immediately erase the fog of silence around race and racism that had hung between us for decades, but it *did* make way for the many conversations we've had since, which have been enlightening and profoundly healing for both of us. It made me realize I'd given up on her, which is itself a form of looking down. And, it restored my respect for how, in the context of committed relationships, people can and do continue to grow and change over time.

We won't always be so fortunate as to have the people

who harm us, whether directly or indirectly, come back to us and spontaneously apologize for what they did or didn't do. Because many of the harms we experience in relationships with loved ones are unintentional, the people who have caused us harm might not even know they've done so. What seems totally obvious to us may have missed the other person completely.

If it feels safe, and if our friendship is strong, going directly to the person who hurt us and sharing what we experienced can open the path forward. It's simple, but not necessarily easy, to start with something like, "When I saw/heard/felt you _____ (do this), I felt _____ (this way about it)." It's simple, but not necessarily easy, to listen to their response and then to make a request: "In the future, I'd like _____ (this instead)." What a huge act of friendship: to respect someone who has harmed us enough to trust that they can actually bear to hear about it, and to respond with friendship in return.

I know that expressing how I've felt harmed can open a whole floodgate of emotion in me. Sharing something that didn't work for me, requesting a change in future behavior— these things fall under the category of setting healthy boundaries. Because setting boundaries feels vulnerable, we can get angry that we even have to do it, frustrated that our friends don't *already know* how we want to be treated. Of course, anger is a totally appropriate response to feeling hurt and then feeling like we have to be the ones to bring it up. Making friends with ourselves in these moments—noticing when there's agitation or discomfort in our bodies or harshness in our minds, and then doing our best to be nonjudgmental and compassionate with ourselves—this is how our practice can help us tolerate the vulnerability of vocalizing that we've been hurt, asking for what we need, and seeing if our friend can meet those needs.

When it comes to addressing harm without looking down on each other, the Buddha's principles of spiritual friendship encourage a radical turn toward tending the relational wound. It's a practice that is wholly unlike the crime and punishment approach that sanctions harm as restitution for harm, and the belief that doing so can bring us peace. The dharma way is much more akin to restorative justice, a process rooted in Indigenous wisdom that is less concerned with punishing an offender and more concerned with understanding the effects of harm and conflict for all involved as well as uncovering the patterns that led to that harm in the first place.[31] Restorative justice asks questions like, *What was the precise nature of the harm that occurred? What are the needs that arose as a result of the harm?* And perhaps most importantly, *Whose obligation is it to meet those needs?* To answer those questions, we must engage in a process of self-reflection that strengthens the love and wisdom we cultivate within a meditative life.

Forgiveness is not something we do alone, looking down on the person who has harmed us as if from a mountaintop of spiritual attainment. As with compassion, forgiveness is an intimate exchange between equals. In the best of times, it is the fruition of a process of engagement in which the person who has been harmed is safe enough to fully express their experience, and the person who caused that harm acknowledges their behavior *and* takes action toward change.[32] Sometimes, for some harms, it's possible to forgive only after we see that the change has been carried out. Sometimes, for some harms, we may be able to come to peace around a hurtful experience *even if* forgiveness still doesn't feel possible.

What do we do if the person who harmed us isn't available to hear what we have to say? Or, if they don't acknowledge their behavior or won't change? What I love about meditation is that, through practice, we have the opportunity to meet some of the needs for ourselves that weren't met by others. Deep listening, patience, acceptance, affirmation, a gentle, warm, committed presence. Treating ourselves really, really well in our meditation practice is one way of tapping into the sense that we deserve to be treated really, really well off the cushion too. When we attend to what hurts with care, moment after moment, a new connective tissue forms within us, covering the places that feel broken with a strong balm of wholeness and love.

There's something about having confidence in our capacity for self-healing after harm that makes us more available for the healing that can come through relationship. When the process of repair begins with inner friendship, then our peace of mind doesn't hinge on the words or actions of others. If we're not demanding it or depending on it, we may be better able to receive a heartfelt apology when and if it comes, and to recognize whatever transformation comes after it.

Of course, restoration comes in many forms. It comes in moments when we turn to comfort an old hurt and realize it doesn't hurt so much anymore. It comes in creative expression, in moments of dance, song, or visual art when what's inside us becomes seen, heard, and shared. It comes in healthy relationships, in times when we're finally able to give and receive all the love we need. It comes through the natural world, attuning with the lessons of trees, animals, bodies of water, and soft spots on the earth. It comes by way of mystery, be it divine intervention or cosmic coincidence. And, it can come through justice, through a transformation in society that corrects the harms of the past and present, and sets us firmly on the path to a harmonious future.

WHEN WE WITNESS HARM

Our dominant day-to-day experience of harm may be neither as perpetrator nor as survivor of harm, but instead as a *witness* to the harm that exists all around us. Hearing a couple shouting at each other in the next apartment. Meeting the eyes of a child who was just harshly disciplined in a grocery store. Seeing a video of another police shooting pop up on your social media feed. Being aware of immigrants and refugees camped out at borders and detained in cages. As we enlarge our practice of radical friendship to include all beings everywhere, how are we to respond to the hurts that don't affect us directly, that we haven't caused directly, but that break our hearts?

How can we, in radical friendship, show up for the liberation of people we don't even know?

Our world may not be more unjust than it was at the time of the Buddha. But having access to information from the far corners of the world means we are more aware of injustice than we ever could have been back then. The flood of images from near and far can overload our senses and make us feel relegated to the role of bystanders—watching people we care about suffer and feeling unable to stop it. The frustration of powerlessness can, if it goes on too long, sink into hopeless indifference. If we feel we can't do anything about what we see, we might decide it's better just to focus on ourselves, and maybe our close circle of friends or family, and close our eyes to the rest.

In socially engaged Buddhist traditions, the practice of consciously being in direct contact with the suffering in our world is called *bearing witness*. It is the same radical shift toward tending the wounds in our hearts, but expanded to the heart of society. When we intentionally bear witness to the harms of discrimination, poverty, addiction, disease, or hunger, we subvert our instinctual response to turn away from what we fear could happen to us if we get too close. If circumstances were different—if we were born to a different family, with a different mental or physical makeup, with a different gender or skin color, in a different country or class—we could absolutely be in the other person's shoes. Recognizing that can open us into the truth of selflessness, the truth that our experience in this life has very little to do with our specialness or individual merits and very much to do with circumstances that could have easily been otherwise.

When I first learned about bearing witness as a practice of socially engaged Buddhism, I was not impressed. I was annoyed. The whole thing sounded distant and remote to me, like the stereotype of the detached, navel-gazing meditator who removes themselves from the cares of the world and its people. *We don't need more people to just sit there and watch,* I thought. *We need more people who are prepped and ready to do something.*

What I now understand is that this process of bearing witness in a sustained and conscious way is the exact activity that makes it possible to take wise action. If we can't tolerate the discomfort of bearing witness with open hearts, we will ultimately act in haste—not so much to interrupt the harm, but to relieve our own discomfort at witnessing it. The actions we take from that place may serve others in a superficial way, but mostly they serve to relieve our feeling of embarrassment at not being able to help.

Our willingness to bear witness is an important part of being in equal relationship with those we care about, especially when they are down-and-out in some way. It is equally important that we don't just *stay* witnesses. In an interdependent universe such as ours, there is no such thing as a bystander. Bearing witness is a practice of clearly seeing suffering or harm and deeply feeling into the truth of those experiences. That moment of clear sight is the end of denial. We must use it as a springboard for compassionate action: action that interrupts cycles of harm, either by addressing the needs that the harm created, or by preventing the harm from happening in the first place.

Over the last few years, there's been revelation after revelation of ongoing sexual abuse within several Buddhist communities I used to practice with. There was a stretch of a few months where I had a hard time even opening my emails. I wouldn't receive one for a few days, and then several would arrive at once. *Kate, I'm overwhelmed, not sure how to process this, where to go, what to do, when can we talk?* My body ached, reading them. I laid in bed, waiting for something more useful to say than *Me too, honey. Me too.*

I talked to a lot of people in the months that followed. Former students and employees of the accused teachers and leaders got in touch to process their grief. I felt honored that they reached out to do so with me. Friends and colleagues who, like me, had taught alongside some of these teachers, got on calls and shared stories, trying to piece together what we had missed. I was haunted in particular by my interactions with a benefactor of one of the organizations I'd worked for. I saw him at least once a year at our holiday parties, and even more as I moved into leadership there. He was pushy with his views about how our projects should run. He was equally pushy with his body—hugging too long, grabbing my hands, or wrapping his arm around my waist, casually but firmly, without invitation. I thought he was awkward and creepy. But because he came with the approval of teachers and community I trusted, I'd bracketed my gut reactions and laughed at his bad jokes instead.

This was just one of several cases where I bore witness to harm caused by colleagues and friends, and then rationalized it away. And this, I think, is how communities become complicit in the abuse of power. We excuse behavior we *know* deep down isn't right because the offender comes highly recommended, or has done so much good in their lives, or because we have something to gain by being close to them. No one else is raising a fuss, so we don't either. When the truth finally comes out, as it almost always does, it feels like we're waking up from deep, disturbing sleep—disoriented, a bit confused, but relieved to be finally awake.

When the people I'd been in community with started coming forward with stories of harassment, assault, and abuse, I wondered about what my role *could* have been in interrupting it. I recognized how tragically low my expectations had been concerning the people who had committed these harms. I realized just how much I *expected* people in power to abuse it in some way. When I witnessed them pushing the line, there was a part of me that just felt glad they weren't blatantly crossing it, at least not in my view. I looked down on them in that way, by not demanding better from them.

I needed accountability too. We all did.

When we fear conflict in our relationships, it's usually because we don't have a process in place to meet and manage those conflicts. And, when there are accountability issues, it's the same—there's often no structure in place that can support safety, dignity, and connection for all people involved while addressing the impacts of harm and the systems that made that harm inevitable. The fear is that if we take responsibility for our part, we'll lose everyone.

In the years since these incidents came to light, I've been profoundly inspired by visions of community accountability articulated within the transformative justice movement. Transformative justice is a political framework and approach that seeks to respond to violence without creating more violence and/or engaging in harm reduction to lessen the violence.[33] It is especially focused on transforming systems in which harm repeatedly happens, and in building new systems that produce different results than the ones we currently have.

I've been especially inspired by the notion of "accountability pods" articulated by the Bay Area Transformative Justice Collective. In the times of global pandemic, we started using the word "pod" to refer to a group of people who were trusting each other to hold the same standards of care, and with whom we could take off our masks. Really, accountability pods aren't so different. As Mia Mingus describes them, "Your pod is made up of the people that you would call on if violence, harm or abuse happened to you; or the people that you would call on if you wanted support in taking accountability for violence, harm or abuse that you've done; or if you witnessed violence or if someone you care about was being violent or being abused."[34] They are radical friendships in that when we enter into them, we go beyond surface-level interaction and ask that our friend support us through the hardest of times, with the confidence they can do so and not lose sight of our bodhicitta along the way. It's a conversation that reminds me of what a Christian leader once described to me as the establishment of "spiritual consent" in his community. Essentially, they agree to witness one another and to speak to their friend directly if they see their shared ethical standards being stretched or disregarded. With love, they promise to hold themselves and each other in integrity, and to welcome reflections and feedback about how they're doing with that.

The key to this kind of accountability is in relationships that are forged and clarified *before* harm happens, ideally. The practice of pod mapping, of identifying the people close to us who we trust to support us in case of emergency, can be tender and revealing. As Mingus notes in her "Pod Mapping Worksheet," we may only be able to come up with a couple of people we can trust to be with us in this way.[35] We may find that the people we can count on to support us when we are harmed are different than the ones who can show up for us when we are the ones who cause it, or when we are witnessing harm and don't know what to do about it. We may recognize that some of our friendships need some further cultivation to become the accountability partnerships we wish for. Having taken an inventory of the relationships we already have, we can use our radical friendship practices to develop them so that they might eventually be solid enough to depend on in a crisis.

I've said it before and I'll say it again: true compassion is a relationship between equals. To hold a perpetrator in compassion is to regard them as fully capable of taking accountability for their actions. They may be at their personal low point, but we must not look down on them by letting them off the hook. If we are a part of their support team, we can gather around them and remind them of the best parts of who they are, and encourage them to live up to their highest potential by doing what it takes to listen to the people they've harmed. We can keep reminding them of is what is needed from them and make every effort to call them into a circle of love that can help them to tell the truth, to take responsibility for their behavior. We can coauthor with them a plan for change that we can accompany them in as they carry it out. In the end, no one can make someone else be accountable for their actions. But, we can let our awareness and our love propel us into being willing participants.

We all need people we can count on in this way because until we are all completely enlightened, we'll continue to cause, experience, and witness harm probably all our lives. The radical possibility of accountability is that we can come *even deeper* into relationship with one another as we support one another to heal, or take to responsibility, or to take action. It means we'll get better at earlier identifying and addressing subtle patterns of harm before they turn into big stinking messes. When we inevitably experience harm, whatever side of it we happen to be on, we will know it is not itself a condition for being isolated from our friends or banished from our communities.

In radical friendship, it is possible to create worlds where being imperfect is not a threat to our belonging. And, we can live inside of these worlds together where it is possible to be both 100 percent accountable and 100 percent free.

PRACTICE
Equanimity

Equanimity is a translation of the Pali word *uppekha*, which means "to look over," as if from a mountain. It's not so much looking down from that mountain as it is looking across, as if you are surveying a great landscape where you can see the interweaving causes and conditions that led to the present moment, as well as all the present-moment actions that are shaping the future. Equanimity is the heart of love that is turned toward wisdom, able to hold the truth of suffering, the truth of change, the unfathomable workings of cause and effect, and the fact that we're not always able to control circumstances of our lives and world. It's the heart that is able to be in touch with all these things and can continue to love anyway.

In a world where to be a radical friend means to witness not only joy and connection but also heartbreak and sorrow, equanimity is a form of love that can help us relate to the ups and downs of life with balance. When it's perfected, equanimity results in a courageous and resilient heart. It's love with a lot of space, and that spaciousness makes it steady and stable, with lots of room for individuals and relationships to grow.

Equanimity contains the sense that just as each person is imbued with a sacred seed of bodhicitta, so too does society hold a kind of basic goodness at its core—even as injustice remains a daily reality. Like our individual bodies, our social bodies and social systems will tend toward well-being with the right support. Equanimity is being able to recognize the current social and political conditions as they are and, at the same time, to know deeply the liberatory possibilities we can imagine in the future.

One way of practicing equanimity is to embody it, by "meditating as a mountain." As you prepare for your meditation practice, find a comfortable way to arrange your body, closing or softening your eyes and resting your hands. Imagine that the lower part of your body is not separate from the earth but rather deeply connected to and emerging from it. See if you can feel that the base of your body is very wide, and as you trace your awareness slowly upward from the lower half of your body, imagine that your mountain body gets taller and slightly narrower until you reach the peak of the mountain at the top of your head. Imagine that, at this peak, the air is cool, clear, and crisp, and that there is a 360-degree view all around. Maybe you can feel your breath coming and going in your body and imagine that it is the wind, swirling around and within the earthy structure of your mountain body. Perhaps you can access the sense of having been here on this spot on the earth for a long time, having weathered many seasons in your lifetime already and having the confidence that you will see many, many more.

You can stay like this, deepening into the grounded energy of your body as you gather your attention around the feeling of breathing. You can also include this felt sense in your other heart meditations to help stabilize yourself when you feel overwhelmed and out of balance.

Another way of practicing equanimity is to use a phrase-based practice with a visualization. In this practice, the phrases become the home base for your attention, the place you come back to whenever you get distracted and invite your mind to rest. The equanimity phrases don't sound as warm as the metta practice of loving-kindness found in the first chapter, so it's important when offering them to do so with warmth and love. These phrases are not a way of putting people out of our hearts; they're a way of establishing healthy boundaries and the appropriate amount of space, so that both we and the people we care about can express our innate bodhicitta.

To start, find your comfortable meditation position. You can even begin with the mountain meditation already described as a way to settle in. Then, bring to mind someone you care about, maybe someone you have a tendency to feel you need to fix or save. Picture them in your mind's eye in as much detail as possible and take them in from the widest possible view. See this person as a child, a teenager, in the middle of their life, as an elderly person. Reflect on the many joys and sorrows they have experienced in their lives so far, as well as the many ups and downs that lie ahead of them. Know that they have both harmed others and been harmed themselves, knowingly and unknowingly, through words, thoughts, and deeds. Let your heart shine on them in the spirit of radical friendship, loving them through all the complexity and respecting their innate capacity to meet the circumstances of their lives. Like a beam from your heart to theirs, offer them the following phrases (or another one that helps you access the feeling of equanimity).

All beings have their own journey.
May you have peace with your journey.

As you recite the phrases, notice how it feels in your mind, heart, and body to send these phrases of equanimity. Repeat the process of visualizing the person and sending the phrase in your thoughts for several minutes.

Now bring your attention to yourself in this moment, just as you are. Check in with your internal landscape. Does this feel like a high point in your life, a low point, or somewhere in between? Are you feeling connected, or are you feeling separate? Worthy or unworthy? Notice the tendency of the mind to project its present experience into the future or the past, to create the perception that we've always been this way and always will be. Widen your view to look across your life and consider all the loves and losses that you have experienced, the unexpected turns of fate and fortune. Whatever is happening now is, in some ways, an inheritance from the past, and the future will be created by how we show up today. Holding this broad awareness, offer yourself these phrases as a gesture of friendship to yourself, and let your heart rest in the glow.

All beings have their own journey.
May I have peace with my journey.

CONCLUSION

Several years into my meditation practice, I started to get a little antsy. As a young meditator I'd come into the practice squirmy, and I thought my restlessness had calmed down over years of letting all that energy swirl and settle. This practice has its cycles though, and in time I found myself once again coming around the bend of wanting to do *any thing but sit*. I signed up for an arts retreat led by Arawana Hayashi, a much-loved Buddhist teacher who had also been a dancer and choreographer for decades. Folks had been urging me to connect with her for years, and I was hopeful that the creative arts could offer a more active way to do mindfulness and contemplation than sitting on my cushion watching my mind.

On retreat, we explored a number of different art forms—dance, sculpture, flower arranging, even eating as a ritual art form. But to my initial dismay, we mostly sat in silent meditation. As we began calligraphy practice, Arawana instructed us—*sit until your hand longs for the brush*. I sat still, noticing, feeling, and waiting. Eventually, my hand began to tingle and pulse, and I knew it was time. *Sit until your brush gets thirsty for the ink*, she said. I sat, and eventually, I felt the tip of the brush become heavy, reaching downward for the bowl of dark ink below.

In the practice of dharma art, she explained, we spend 90 percent of our time cultivating the right mind state for making art—a state of sensitivity, curiosity, and wonder. From that state, in the remaining 10 percent of the time, our artwork emerges the way a flower blooms—effortlessly, in perfect form.

Friendship is an art form too. In this book, we've spent the majority of our time contemplating radical friendship as an attitude of heart and mind, one that we can organize ourselves around as we view and navigate our relationships and our world. Meditation, reflection, journaling—these practices cultivate our minds and hearts and give us confidence that we'll know when our hand begins to long for the brush. Our job is to be willing to follow that sensation, to pick it up when it's time to make our move, to reach out in friendship. To begin, or to begin again.

All this to say that the *Mitta Sutta* isn't just a list of principles that are nice to think about. It's a *guide* for aligning our thoughts, speech, and actions with our hearts' intent, allowing us to connect in ways that are real, mutually beneficial, and disruptive to the socially proscribed ways of relating to ourselves and to one another. It's a series of directions for how to put our insights into action. Practicing these teachings have radically changed all my relationships—with elders and young folks, with neighbors and colleagues, with strangers, with myself, and with various circles of friends and family. Radical friendship doesn't mean we won't still have "mean girl on the playground" moments, when we find ourselves unexpectedly face-to-face with someone else's unconsciousness or ignorance—even someone we thought was a friend. What the practice means is that we need not go through those moments alone. That in the cultivation of authentic friendships we can find healing for the suffering of separation that has been passed down to us and lived through us.

From the Buddhist perspective, enlightenment sometimes happens in a single revelatory event. But more often, enlightenment comes as a result of incremental change, a series of chops in the trunk of an old tree that gradually make it weaker until it eventually topples and comes down. Our love for each other is like a million tiny axes to the great tree of suffering and confusion.

Until complete and total liberation, I think one of our best strategies for embodying enlightenment is to love each other well. In the Zen traditions, it's said that another way of describing enlightenment is *intimacy with all things*. It is the consciousness of our closeness and our longing to maintain and deepen this closeness. That is the expression of the awakening heart.

It will take a mass movement to transform the most pressing social and political issues we face today. Friendship alone can't disrupt mass incarceration, end racial profiling and police brutality, interrupt a culture of sexual violence, or provide quality, accessible health care for all. What friendship *can* do is reveal the ways we all suffer under systemic injustice and ignite the longing for real liberation—not only spiritually, but also socially and politically. Friendship can lift our energy and sustain our spirits such that we can work together for the legislative and policy reforms that would restore equity across our societies in a tangible way.

Radical friendship alone might not save the world, but it can save our lives, and it can bolster our spirits long enough for us to do the world-saving, world-building, and world-making work we need to do to pass on something of value to future generations. As we confront crisis after political crisis on a rapidly heating planet, we can only expect that life will get more intense from here on out. In the midst of that intensity, our capacity to befriend our own hearts and bodies will make the difference between shining bright and burning out. Our capacity to give and receive love in all our relationships will make the difference between showing up for each other's liberation out of duty and showing up out of desire—the desire to see each other live and thrive and be truly free. Because it is in the showing up for friendship, our hearts in our hands, that we find our people. And, it is in the showing up for friendship—for the tough conversation, for the big laugh, for the moment of need, for the seeing and being seen, for the mistake and everything after—that our people find us too.

ACKNOWLEDGMENTS

No one writes a book by themselves. *Radical Friendship* was a collective labor of love that blossomed out of many, many sacred relationships. I wrote this book . . .

With the support of the ancestors: the Indian, Thai, Burmese, Tibetan, Japanese, and Chinese Buddhist lineages who held the teachings that have blessed my life; the guidance of my own ancestors of the African Diaspora, the Americas, and Europe; and all the powers of their spiritual lineages, known and unknown to me.

With the blessings and guidance of my teachers, especially: Gina Sharpe, Larry Yang, Lila Kate Wheeler, Arawana Hayashi, Thanissara, Kittisaro, Phillip Moffitt, and Ruth King.

With the brilliant reflections and patient nurturing of my literary guides: Lisa Weinert, Alisha Acquaye, Rachel Neumann, Jeanann Pannasch, Mia Herndon, and Ericka Phillips. With the books that this one aspires to be in company with and the authors who wrote them: *Radical Dharma* by Reverend angel Kyodo williams, Lama Rod Owens, and Jasmine Syedullah; *Radical Acceptance* and *Radical*

Compassion by Tara Brach; *Mindful of Race* by Ruth King; *Emergent Strategy* by adrienne maree brown; and *Dharma, Color, and Culture* edited by Ryūmon H. Baldoquín. With gratitude for Sarah Stanton, Audra Figgins, and the whole team at Shambhala Publications who helped make these ideas into a book.

With the gentle, generous support of organizations where I've facilitated, taught, and learned: Rubin Museum of Art, the Omega Institute, the Kripalu Center for Yoga & Health, Spirit Rock Meditation Center, the Institute of Contemporary Art of Philadelphia, the Interdependence Project, New York Insight Meditation Center, the Presencing Institute, and Insyte Partners.

With the unconditional love of my family: Ann, Don, Emily, Laurel, Jonathan, Karen, Bill, and all the rest of the Johnsons, Brooks, Morells, and DeClues. With my beloved Rolando Hernandez Rodriguez Brown, best dance partner ever, and with Purple Ray Kolker-Brown, who has taught me more about friendship than I can ever say.

With the inspiration, cheer, sparkle, and shine of all my radical friends, with gratitude for our many conversations that echo through these pages, especially Sara Jimenez, Isabel Wilder, Chanel Matsunami Govreau, Ruby Amanze, Shantrelle P. Lewis, La Sarmiento, Zavé Martohardjono, Dawn Haney, Max Airborne, Katie Loncke, LiZhen Wang, Beatrice Anderson, Rolf Gates, Erin Selover, DaRa Williams, Helen Kim, Sandra Kim, Aaron Goggans, Lezlie Frye, Jacoby Ballard, Carinne Luck, Sebene Selassie, Matthew Hepburn, Jozen Tamori Gibson, Danielle Saint Louis,

Acknowledgments

Louije Kim, Leslie Booker, Victoria Cary, Konda Mason, and all my dharma siblings at Spirit Rock.

With you. I can't wait to hear what you're thinking, feeling, and doing in the realms of radical friendship. Thank you for reading. Let's keep in touch.

NOTES

1. Kate Johnson, "The Dharma of Difference," speech, August 17, 2013, Buddhist Geeks Conference, Boulder, CO.
2. Alice Walker, *In Search of Our Mothers' Gardens: Womanist Prose* (New York: Houghton Mifflin Harcourt Publishing, 1983), xi.
3. Thanissaro Bhikku, trans. *Uppadha Sutta*, Samyutta Nikaya 45.2, 1997 https://www.accesstoinsight.org/tipitaka/sn/sn45/sn45.002.than.html
4. *Sutta* means "thread" in the ancient Indian language of Pali, the language many of the Buddha's teachings were recorded. This thread of wisdom called the *Mitta Sutta* (not to be confused with the *Metta Sutta*, which offers instructions on lovingkindness) is pulled from the Anguttara Nikaya, which is a collection of things that the Buddha taught, categorized by number.
5. Sonya Renee Taylor, *The Body Is Not an Apology: The Power of Radical Self-Love* (Oakland, CA: Berrett-Koehler, 2018), 40.
6. Cynthia Brown et al., *Dismantling Racism: 2016 Workbook*. dR Works, https://resourcegeneration.org/wp-content/uploads/2018/01/2016-dRworks-workbook.pdf, 28–35.

7. Brown et al., *Dismantling Racism*, 28–35.

8. Funie Hsu, "We've Been Here All Along," *Lion's Roar*, May 17 2017, https://www.lionsroar.com/weve-been -here-all-along/.

9. Jenny Anderson, "Loneliness Is Bad for Our Health. Now Governments Around the World Are Finally Tackling It," *Quartz*, October 9, 2018, https://qz.com/1413576/ loneliness-is-bad-for-our-health-now-governments -around-the-world-are-finally-tackling-the-problem/.

10. Naz Beheshti, "The Detrimental Effect of Loneli-ness on Your Health and What You Can Do about It," *Forbes*, May 31, 2019, https://www.forbes.com/sites/ nazbeheshti/2019/05/31/the-detrimental-effect-of -loneliness-on-your-health-and-what-you-can-do -about-it/.

11. Prentis Hemphill, "Healing Justice Is How We Can Sustain Black Lives," *Huffington Post*, February 7, 2017, www.huffpost.com/.

12. Thanissaro Bhikkhu, trans. *Itivuttaka Sutta 26*, Novem-ber 30, 2013, https://www.accesstoinsight.org/tipitaka/ kn/iti/iti.1.001-027.than.html.

13. Mia Mingus, "Wherever You Are Is Where I Want to Be: Crip Solidarity," *Leaving Evidence*, May 3, 2010, https:// leavingevidence.wordpress.com/2010/05/03/where -ever-you-are-is-where-i-want-to-be-crip-solidarity/.

14. Mushim Patricia Ikeda, "I Vow Not to Burn Out," *Lion's Roar*, June 13, 2019, www.lionsroar.com/i-vow-not-to -burn-out/.

15. Dedrick Asante-Muhammed, Chuck Collins, Josh Hoxie, and Emanuel Nieves, *The Ever-Growing Gap* (Washington, DC: Institute for Policy Studies and CFED, August 2016), http://www.ips-dc.org/report-ever-growing-gap/.

16. Johnella LaRose, personal interview with the author, February 16, 2017.

17. Thanissaro Bhikkhu, trans. *Sappurisadana Sutta: A Person of Integrity's Gift*, AN 5.148, July 3, 2010, https://www.accesstoinsight.org/tipitaka/an/an05/an05.148.than.html.

18. bell hooks, *All About Love: New Visions* (New York: Harper Collins, 2001), 4.

19. *Karaniya Metta Sutta: The Buddha's Words on Loving-kindness*, Sn 1.8, trans. The Amaravati Sangha, November 2, 2013, https://www.accesstoinsight.org/tipitaka/kn/snp/snp.1.08.amar.html.

20. I learned these phrases from the Buddhist teacher Larry Yang.

21. Samyutta Nikaya 56.11, trans. Thanissaro Bhikku, https://www.accesstoinsight.org/tipitaka/sn/sn56/sn56.011.than.html.

22. Claire Pomeroy. "Loneliness is Harmful to Our Nation's Health." *Scientific American*, 20 March 2019. https://blogs.scientificamerican.com/observations/loneliness-is-harmful-to-our-nations-health/.

23. Ajahn Passano and Ajahn Amaro, *The Island: An Anthology of the Buddha's Teachings of Nibbana* (Redwood City, CA: Abhayagiri Monastic Foundation, 2009), 5.

24. Alexis Pauline Gumbs, "Evidence," in *Octavia's Brood*, ed. Walidah Imarisha and adrienne maree brown (Oakland, CA: AK Press, 2015), 9–40.

25. "What is 'Visionary Fiction?' An Interview with Walidah Imarisha," *EAP: The Magazine*, March 31, 2016, http://exterminatingangel.com/eap-the-magazine/what-is-visionary-fiction-an-interview-with-walidah-imarisha/.

26. adrienne maree brown, "attention liberation, attention reparations," *adrienne maree brown*, October 28, 2017, http://adriennemareebrown.net/2017/10/28/attention-liberation-attention-reparations/.

27. *Samyutta Nikaya 45.55*, trans. Piya Tan , http://www.themindingcentre.org/dharmafarer/wp-content/uploads/2010/02/34.12-Yoniso-Manasikara-Sampada-S-s45.55-piya.pdf.

28. Zenju Earthlyn Manuel, *The Way of Tenderness: Awakening through Race, Sexuality, and Gender* (Somerville, MA: Wisdom Publications, 2015), 61.

29. Kittisaro and Thanissara, *Listening to the Heart: A Contemplative Journey to Engaged Buddhism* (Berkeley, CA: North Atlantic Books, 2014), 129.

30. Autumn Brown and adrienne maree brown, "The Practices We Need: #metoo and Transformative Justice Part 2," *The End of the World*, November 7, 2018, www.endoftheworldshow.org/blog/2018/11/7/the-practices-we-need-metoo-and-transformative-justice-part-2.

31. Restorative Justice on the Rise (RJOY). "What is Restorative Justice?" https://restorativejusticeontherise.org/resource-hub/faqs/.

32. Fania Davis, *The Little Book of Race and Restorative Justice: Black Lives, Healing, and US Social Transformation* (New York: Simon and Schuster, 2019), 28–9.

33. Mia Mingus, "Transformative Justice: A Brief Description," *Transform Harm*, https://transformharm.org/transformative-justice-a-brief-description/.

34. Mia Mingus, "Pods and Pod Mapping Worksheet," *Bay Area Transformative Justice Collective*, June 2016, https://batjc.wordpress.com/pods-and-pod-mapping-worksheet/.

35. Mingus, "Pods and Pod Mapping Worksheet."

ABOUT THE AUTHOR

Kate Johnson believes that the practice of wise relationships is a profound spiritual path—one that is high, wide,
and unfathomably deep. She is a passionate meditator, facilitator, and interdisciplinary schoolteacher who has also
been a modern dancer, cocktail waitress, and organizational
development consultant. In the fall of 2020, after a decade
of intensive training and retreat practice in the Insight
Meditation tradition, Kate completed a four-year training and was formally authorized as a Buddhist meditation
teacher at Spirit Rock Meditation Center. These days, she
offers workshops and retreats that integrate meditation,
justice, embodiment, and relational practice. Kate was born
and raised in Chicago and now lives with her family in
Philadelphia, where she can be found exploring with her
kids, sipping tea with friends, and looking for good trouble.
Find her at katejohnson.com and @hellokatejohnson.